ALSO BY MONICA ANDERSON

Chemistry with Kismet:
Journeying into the Self to Heal the Mind

And What If . . . Concepts Challenging the Norm

SOMETHING

SPIRITUALLY

CATCHY

BY

MONICA ANDERSON

Independently Published

By

Monica Anderson: The Kismet Chemist

This is a work of nonfiction. All names have either been changed or included with the express permissions of the peoples named. The events while being true, are that of the perception of the author and do not reflect those of the characters and people in the book. All concepts and ideas presented here are the sole opinion of the author and do not reflect medical or legal advice.

First paperback edition April 2022

Book design by Monica Anderson
Cover Art by Adobe InDesign Stock Photos

ISBN
978-1-7374626-5-1 (hardcover)
978-1-7374626-7-5 (paperback)
978-1-7374626-6-8 (eBook)

This book is dedicated to the people who know, the ones who struggle, and the ones who overcome every time.

Contents

"I tell the truth. It's what I do. [...] And you don't get to take that away from me and call it a lesson."

- Alex Karev, *Grey's Anatomy, Season 2,*
  Episode 22 – The Name of the Game

Brutal Warning

Spirituality saved my life and destroyed all I had ever known. It lifted me from the darkness only to plunge me into the darkest abyss imaginable. It rescued my soul through slaying my ego time and again. I wouldn't change a single thing that happened on the journey. I also am not going to sugarcoat this shit.

It seems too often on this journey people tout how amazing and miraculous the spirituality journey is. My opinion, after the last three years of purging, healing, and continual dark nights of the soul with little to no trips up into the light of happiness, these people lie. Every last one of them. They tell you and me these things.

We believe them.

Why do we do this?

We believe all the candy canes and roses bullshit because when you are one of the souls truly on the path of healing and karmic clearing, you desperately want to believe that at some point you will witness and experience the reality of the hope we continue to hold onto with every fiber of our being.

I am not here to tell you it is easy. I am not here to paint a rosy picture. I am here to be brutally fucking honest about what I have endured and learned on this journey. I will not tell you that it is all rainbows and puppies (though on my journey there was a new puppy – but not without the loss of a beloved pet unexpectedly first).

I am not here to lie.

Why not?

Wouldn't making this journey seem like it ends or brings in wonders unimaginable drive sales?

Of fucking course those things would, but would they help anyone?

No.

It would make me part of the massive problem. At some point, someone needs to tell the damn truth to the people who don't understand or even those who know their souls chose to walk the same kind of path mine did. It is the kind of path that when you are far enough along, and become aware of it, you stop fighting the outside world.

This end to fighting comes when you feel more exhausted than you ever have. It is the kind of exhaustion where you feel like a grand cosmic joke, run over by a bulldozer, and there is nothing left for you to do but lie down and die. The biggest problem you find is you don't even have the will left to die.

It is a special kind of torture, hitting this point. You can't be mad at Spirit/the Universe/God, whatever you call your higher power. You can't be mad at the people in or out of your life, and you know there is only one place your anger is directed: at your own damn soul.

This is the point you have realized your subconscious mind has been constantly battling the darkest enemy - yourself. The part of you that cannot believe your soul chose to crawl, struggle through, and even at times drown in the sheer level of shit you have gone through.

Why – why did it choose this?

To uplevel?

To clear karma?

To help others?

Half the time we don't even find out the why of it. We just have to swallow the goddamn red pill, travel through the rabbit hole, and out of the so-called matrix we are all living in. Once you get out, you realize the journey isn't over. Oh no, it couldn't possibly be quite so simplistic. You've broken out of the conditioned belief there is nothing more than what we are able to experience through our five senses, a feat of wonder in and of itself.

Now, you find yourself in the utmost uncomfortable place in your life. You know, to the core of your being, you have to go to war with every wrong choice in this life and every other one. Not only our own choices, but also our ancestors, soul families, and especially (at least in my case and the case of those who are parents) our children.

I have come to the conclusion (which I am sure it will change and flux in time because life will somehow miraculously turn around just to make all of this seem like pedantic bitching) that my soul is a masochist for karma. Some part of me signed up to endure this bullshit, signed up to endure the traumas, the lack, the struggle, the suffering. Why would it do that? Because of blind faith in its own strength.

Fucking bravado!

So here is your brutal warning: if any of this offends you, if you want to fight against this stance and tell me it is all angels and puffy clouds - Bring it! Either your soul is still trying to get to you and wake you up, or it chose to remain sleeping to this side of the spiritual journey in this lifetime.

Lucky you, but don't shit on the rest of our parades. And believe you me, we deserve parades, ticker tape style, with a giant inflatable Snoopy like the Macy Day Thanksgiving extravagance, where people throw us a freaking bone in life instead of candy.

We deserve to be heard and damn it, I know I am not the only one conquering great unseen feats through this karmic healing journey. If no one else will step up before me to speak the truth of it, then I will be the first.

For those of you who are going to scoff at the karmic aspect of this, I am here to tell you: do not fucking laugh about something you very well may be carrying within your own blood. There are a great many secrets hiding within the world, down to the very genetic makeup within us. I know this from firsthand experience.

It is no joking matter. Not to me. Not to anyone born into a family carrying these things, and not to the world. These secrets are the things keeping the status quo in a continual pattern of war, famine, ignorance, and pain. Do not scoff at what very well may be holding you and your life hostage.

I will gladly open this path of transparency to the warriors, the truest healers, the ones who know and feel the ultimate power within them and NEVER succumb to beating another down nor manipulating for power, but ALWAYS live for their soul because they are seemingly pre-programmed to have ZERO choice on it.

Those are my people.

The ones who want to quit yet can't.

The ones who want relief and still face the shadows head on, every single time.

Half the time I wish I could go back to sleeping, even if it would have killed me at a young age. It has been a heart-wrenching, tearing down of all I believed, forced me to fight for every single sense of groundedness, safety, and security while being attacked left, right, and center by all those who want to take from me for their own use, kind of journey.

If they want to take my light, they need to take the shadows that go right along with them because we live in the world of duality and polarity. You can't take one without the other and frankly I could use a break from them both these days.

Let me tell you, and this is definitely directed at those who are opposed to these words, those who know they have taken from others to serve their own needs and uses without a care for what it did to the other person. Yeah, you, the one that feels uncomfortable right now because you know this is hitting you in a new kind of way.

For you, let me tell you, if you think you can handle taking another's light for yourself, if you think you can handle walking the kind of soul journey these beautiful souls signed up to endure, come back here after ALL your shadows are triggered simultaneously and you have no other option but to face them or watch as your entire life falls down around you.

You really only get one warning that it is coming, if you don't do your due diligence to your soul's calling, life becomes a chaotic tornado of destruction. Let's trigger yours and then you can come back here when you are ready, I'll wait with my popcorn.

HA!

Okay, I'll admit, even to myself I sound jaded and cynical. You know what, I am allowed to feel this. So the fuck are you. I am not the kind of "Spiritual Teacher" who will tell you that your emotions are wrong, and you shouldn't feel them.

I won't even tell you not to attach to them. That shit pisses me off more than I can tell you. Tell an empath to feel without attaching. To feel through every nerve, every fiber, every drop of blood in their body, their emotions or those of others, but don't attach to it. Don't give it a voice, don't give it a place to stand center stage and scream out the anguish. Fuck that!

If you are angry, scream, yell, break shit, make it something physical. If you don't, that is how self-harm is born within an empath. And I guarantee you, all those who cut themselves, playing games like "how deep can I go," it is because they aren't attaching to their emotions enough to give them a voice.

I have too often found a skewed perception of what emotional attachment is when speaking about empathic gifts. It isn't about clinging to something toxic. Do you really think that is what we desire?

We aren't weak!

We are fucking transmuters.

We have to attach to them for a time enough to identify what they are, where they are coming from, and how to heal them.

Attachment is based on perception and intuition; it is sourced from within, and the inner knowing is how we utilize it. It is either a tool of growth or a weapon of destruction. Don't deign to tell those who work with them intimately how we are meant to use attachment to help us work through them.

You all want to know why the collective unconscious has so much darkness swirling in it? It is because we don't allow for the fullness of the human experience.

Emotions are a crucial part of this experience. If we don't feel them fully, don't talk about them, scream them out, and learn how to move in a different way, we feed the repressed emotions from millennia, shoved down and repressed through all the history of mankind.

Just fucking stop.

Just stop doing it.

This is about the truth of the journey. The good, the bad, the ugly. It is about the people I have met, the karmic shit I have waded through, the connections forged and then broken, the injustice and the pain, and the healing and revelations.

It is the raw, real look into what the spiritual community doesn't talk enough about and, in some circles, intentionally avoids. It's the shit I need to pour out of me, so this is for me more than anything. To give a voice to all the moments I have been shoving down because it was the "right way" to do the spiritual life. Welcome to life kids, it's kind of like hell, but there are some fun times thrown in.

Go get some popcorn. Pour a glass of wine if that is what you prefer. Whiskey, if you aren't at the "tame stage," and need something more to take the edge off. Whatever you need. I am not going to tell you to not do it if you believe you are still in need of it. I know that stage, went through it to the other side, and I know it serves its purpose.

Do what you need to do but get ready for a rollercoaster. Hell, maybe by the end of this you'll think, "My life really isn't that hard." Others of you are likely to tell me the one thing that has been continually triggering me from my conditioning, "Your life isn't that bad, there are plenty of people who have it worse, look at (fill in the blank for someone suffering in a different way that you think is worse than my situation)."

Pain and trauma is not a popularity contest. It isn't something to use as a measurement of worth or shortcoming. It is something to help us grow. Don't tell someone else their pain isn't important, and don't diminish yours. Simultaneously, realize we all have traumas and things we perceive in our lives that bring pain into being.

This is not about whose story is more worthy than another, it is not about what third world country is enduring harder times than the friend confiding in you, and it is not about pretending struggle does not exist in the world.

To tell you the truth, I kind of hope there are a lot of you in that second group, the ones who challenge the importance of another's experiences, because this whole book is aimed at people like you.

Why? Why did I choose you for my target audience?

Because you are like me. Master minimizers of your own pain. When you give in to that, you minimize others' pain as well, and this action haunts you. I know because I have done that too. It still haunts me. I work my ass off daily to be sure I do not fall back into those patterns ever again. You can get out of it too.

How fucking egotistical of me. Yet, I own all the shit I did because I see it for what it is: a broken part of my psyche, calling for me to look at it and deal with it, to somehow put the pieces back together or to stitch new patches in. We all deserve a voice no matter the outer perception of others, and there are always going to be those who will tell you to shut up and put up.

They don't want their secret shames to be exposed, they don't want their carefully constructed personas to be challenged by you. Do it anyway. Your voice and your story matter more than their egos.

I keep thinking, if we all think this way, behave this way, believe this way, the manipulators and narcissists will lose their power, and the pressure to change will become so great we will see a Great Transformation instead of this bullshit Great Resignation we are living in.

Shall we get started?

Timeline Jumping

1

Okay, so the title is a little deceiving. This is not quantum jumping, this isn't about timeline shifting. This is going to be jumping through time in my life. It is its own way of timeline jumping. It is something to help put pieces together of why the fuck we are here in the first place. Why I am here.

Also, I have the feeling that the profanity is going to temper down in time, but where I am on my journey right now, there is just a lot of throat clearing. There was a tarot reader who one time said that when we swear, we clear our throat chakras, and it rang ridiculously true for me.

Look! Spiritual lesson!

How about we take a moment before we go through the bullshit of how I got here to clear our throat chakras. I would suggest you don't do this while you are in church, court, a parent-teacher conference, or around tiny human ears . . .

I'll give you a minute to get yourself into a place to do this . . .

Don't worry, don't rush.

I am learning perpetual patience, I can wait . . .

Are you ready yet?!?!

Alright, let's do this!

Repeat after me:

SHIT! FUCK! DAMN!

Okay, now feel free to get creative with it. Scream profanities, scream to the heavens. I literally just saw in my clairvoyance, a shit ton of Spirit Guides all cheering and laughing.

Welcome to finding your voice.

Welcome to how I share my gifts and tell my stories! My gifts and I aren't separable. They and I are one in the same. So when I say what I am hearing, seeing, or feeling, take it how you will, but this is a lesson in learning to let your gifts come naturally. I had to learn that lesson the hard way. Can't define them, don't know how they work logically, I just know they do.

Have you ever found yourself talking about something, or sending a text to someone, and your brain has suddenly flitted off in a completely different direction? Yeah, it happens to me all the time. I usually try my best to come full circle, to bring it back to where I was, but shit do we go on one hell of a journey of tangents when it happens.

Does anyone else do this? Realize halfway through the beginning of something, you no longer have the vision, the words become lost in translation, the meaning, or the purpose behind it drifted away like vapor on the wind, but you can't just fucking quit and walk away.

What good would that do?

That is giving up!

It is caving to the fear and doubt!

No sir, not me, and certainly not you!

Right?

To continue would mean you would have to put your proverbial "big girl/boy panties on" (let's not make this about gender please, for all those out there who prefer gender fluidity, more power to you, but it is a saying my parent's told me, and I am sure their parents did before them as well, it isn't about your comfort level, but rather my own personal conditioning). Who the hell wants to figure out their whole life in the two minutes it takes to decide, *am I really going to give up on myself and my dreams again?*

Do you understand what I am talking about?

If you do, then you seem to understand me on a level few do.

THANK FUCKING GOD!

I don't want to give you too much credit, honestly, because when I do that, I end up saying something, and then you say something, and then I get defensive, and the whole thing falls apart. We're going to do what my former custody lawyer told me once: KISS – Keep It Simple Stupid.

I'm not convinced there is a single part of this journey that is simple in nature, but what the hell, let's try to keep it simple, shall we? Alright, so let's jump back in time.

It was the end of July 2020. Ironically, while the rest of the world was worrying about whether or not they would get COVID, whether their rights were being violated by being required to wear a mask outside of the house, I was worrying about whether or not my children would be heard in court, if they would be forced to return to their abusive father's house, and whether or not the whole mess would end with a positive outcome.

I have often wondered if it was Spiritual Ego getting in my way. Blind faith my spirit guides and spirit would never allow something as seemingly heinous as my children being forced to go back to a home where both parents were hurting them emotionally, mentally, physically, and as my ex-husband (nicknamed George in my first book *Chemistry with Kismet*) asserted to his friends and family -sexually.

You know, on this note, I would like to state just how sickening it is to know George was running around telling people I was a terrible person because I was accusing Wendy of sexually assaulting our children. All the lies he told about false accusations being made, despite the fact I never once stated anything of the sort, nor did I ever put that into court documents. No, it was not I who made that claim, he did.

Bitch fest this may be, the point in mentioning the erroneous nature of that incident is not about George. In fact, if you will but shift your perspective a bit, you will begin to understand a truth: nothing I am writing is about the other people, nor about me.

Everything contained in these pages are about you. This whole fucking book, my messy story, it is about you. It is all about how you have endured these or similar struggles. It is about the loneliness and desperation you have felt, and the offering I am making to show you: *you have not suffered alone, you are not the only one, and you can step up, speak up, and move forward.*

In this situation, what would you do?

What did you do?

Somehow, I have found we have all been on the receiving end of someone else's negativity, lies, and projections. We are all faced with a moment of truth from within. Are we going to engage in the exact same behavior we are so hurt and/or offended by?

No, no we aren't. At least, I didn't. Maybe I should have. Sometimes I have wondered what would have happened if I hadn't stayed so silent during that whole debacle. Yet, I did not want my children to endure having two parents at war with one another. If I were able to remain calm, keep my pains and worries coming at me from their father private, continue to remind them they are loved, then perhaps I could prevent the damage taking hold of them.

There is no telling at this point what I should and shouldn't have done. I am still proud of myself for not caving to the same behavior. For choosing to be on the offensive rather than defensive. Sometimes it is the hardest actions we take where we find ourselves the utmost proud of what we have accomplished. Those are the moments the world will never really see. Where were we before I went off on this tangent? Oh yes! I remember...

As the world stood on the sidelines of the beginning of a pandemic, I found myself lost in the world of text and Facebook messages dating back to 2007 between George and me. As though I had somehow teleported back to that time, all the same feelings began to build up inside of me like a slow cacophony rising from the very deepest parts of my being.

Right in front of me in black and white I found myself witnessing once more the horrors of the marriage from which I had escaped. Knowing my children were beginning to suffer from the same horrors in a new, more upsetting manner consumed my being. This is where my timeline jumping really starts to matter.

2

I could go back to my Kundalini awakening in June and July of 2011. Glimpse the time it began getting easier in August of 2011. The visions, the pressure, the pain, and the way George was drugging me, thinking I was blind to his actions. I could go back there, but that was a precursor to the long days and nights I spent reading every interaction between myself and George, and even at times Wendy.

All the threats, the fears they were once able to fabricate internally which manifested externally within my life, all of the power I gave to them sat right in front of me on my computer screen. It was a sickening thing for me to see. It became all-consuming like a train wreck you just can't look away from.

Ugh! Okay, so I admit, this is becoming less likely to be anything I could put out into the world and more like I just need to get all the negative bitching out of my system, but you never know? Maybe I will grow the cajones and let the whole world know just how depraved these two are. Let the world see the flaws and errors in the so-called "Justice System" we all rely on to keep us and especially our children safe.

Fuck.

Someone needs to expose it all to the world. The problem I am facing with all of this is, for those who cannot see it: if I publish this, I equally look like a whining, bitch of an ex-wife as well as sound like a victim.

Fuck all of that.

Are you finding a pattern here yet? This is not the first time I have contested my own endeavor here. When we are bringing hard truths into the light of day, choosing to share our stories and speak our experiences, every fear of repercussions, ostracization, and condemnation flood to the front of our minds.

I am no different. I have lived many years in a state of fighting my own inner fears, and those I allowed to be planted within my subconscious mind from the words of others. I choose continually to step beyond the shadows of those fears and doubts, and to speak these things out into the world. It wasn't always like this for me, this continual notion of it being safe to speak out.

This changed drastically for me during the summer of 2021. My kids had been forced to resume visitation with their father (spoilers), and my daughter texted me panicking. The visit prior, her stepmother, Wendy, had seemed to go a bit off the deep end.

It is more than a little disconcerting when you receive a phone call from your 12-year-old daughter whispering, "Mom, something isn't right. Wendy just told me to get ready to leave two hours early. She had a look in her eyes. I am scared she is going to do something crazy. What if she kills us?" Followed promptly by the phone call disconnecting.

Call back.

No answer.

Text.

No answer.

Time after time I tried to contact her until I received a text message saying "I just broke. I can't do this anymore."

At this point I had called her father no less than seven times. Attempted to contact her stepmother another five, and to no avail. I was left with one option. I had to call the police and report the entire situation. They did a welfare check.

As the officer pulled up, my daughter was being screamed at by her father because she hadn't treated him well nor planned anything special for him for Father's Day. The officer asked my daughter if she felt safe in her father's home.

Her response, "Sometimes."

He asked if she felt safe right then, and it was a resounding, "No."

This was when her father decided to tell the officer that I was just a crazy ex-wife. I was making things up. And rolling his eyes, shrugging his shoulders, he said, "You know how ex-wives can get."

No one is a victim unless they choose to be, and me, well I am no victim. At least not anymore. I used to be. I really was. Alcoholic, sad, depressed, and couldn't fight for myself and what was right for me nor my children.

That was my past.

I suppose that is one of the best things spirituality brought to me. It took the victim out of me. Though it wasn't done the easy way. No it wasn't all "change your thoughts and change your life." Instead it was a slam you in the face with the reality of how weak you have been kind of wake-up call from the universe. (Me and the Universe have quite the sordid history of loving and detesting each other in equal measure – I am working on it.)

It was the following visit things truly brought me to the breaking point of my silence. I was already concerned after the way the prior visit had gone, and I received another text from my daughter. She was in a full panic. Her father was taking her cell phone away nightly.

At the time she was in therapy, and it was a condition of her therapy for her to have her phone with her. It was a safety net. Without it, she had no way to call for help, no way to contact anyone if things in her father's house took a turn. It was a night burned in my memory.

I informed her father of his going against the therapy parameters. He told me he didn't give a shit. His house, his rules. My daughter facetimed me and she was having a full-blown anxiety attack. As I was attempting to help her regulate her breathing, she told me she was terrified to be there, and wanted to come home. My hands were tied by the justice system. We all knew it. We were all there in the courtroom.

Her father came into her room and started yelling about getting off the phone with me. They had talked to me enough; they didn't need to be on the phone with me. I asked him to have a discussion with me and him and the kids. An attempt to coparent and talk things out.

He refused and stormed out and slammed the door. The fear on my daughter's face was like nothing I had ever seen before. As a mother, I was completely helpless in the situation. All I could do was try to assure her it would be okay; she would be okay. It was during this comment he stormed back in and started yelling for her to get off the phone.

As my daughter began to hyperventilate, her Conversion Disorder in full form as her body was involuntarily jerking, I could see fear and pain commingling. I tried to keep her focus on me. This was something we had practiced and worked on for the past year. We had this system down; a few minutes and she would have been able to shift out of where she was and back into a state of calm.

A few minutes was all we needed. It was not what was afforded. George yelled, "Hang up the fucking phone!"

I responded, "I am not going to hang up the phone until she is calmed down."
As David and I sat in our bedroom, the screen paused and all we could hear was my daughter screaming help as though her life depended on it. We could hear George grunting and a scuffle. I looked at David terrified and told him to call the police. That was when the line went dead.

Another call to the police. Another welfare check. Yet, George and Wendy were prepared for it. Wendy called the police and reported our daughter as being an "uncontrollable teenager trying to run away." A mark on her juvenile record.

What they weren't aware of was the fact I had called back, and my daughter answered. My husband and I recorded the conversation that night. For at least fifteen minutes George and Wendy berated my daughter, telling her this was all her fault, she was going to have to tell the police what she did wrong. It was on her shoulders, they expected her to explain it to the police.

Would you believe in the state of North Dakota, if you do not put your child in the hospital, or cause them harm which risks their life, it isn't considered abuse? My daughter had bruises and deep psychological trauma from that night, but because of a false police report from Wendy, and the century code in North Dakota, the legal system justified his abuse.

This is one of the many problems in society. Our children suffer at the hands of the people meant to love them and protect them, and the justice system does nothing. An abuser receives justification by the law to harm innocent children. And we wonder why there are so many broken children, broken adults, why there is so much darkness in the world?

It is there because we blind ourselves to it, or because, those who have been in the helpless parent role, like me, believe there is no point anymore. Not even the systems in place for protection afford that. A week after that night, I spoke with the first officer who had reported to George's house. He wasn't the one who reported the second time, though I truly wish he were.

He told me the reason he became a police officer was because of parents like George and Wendy. He grew up with those parents and knew how skewed the system was, and he endeavored to be one who did it differently. He did everything he was able for my children, and there is no love between George and the officer, but one going against the whole, well those stories are rare for the one overcoming.

It was this situation that opened my eyes. It opened my throat chakra too. I stopped allowing for the lies to continue. If I was asked, I told the truth. I gave my children the safe space to speak their truth, and I chose to speak my own truth. Enough is enough. It is kind of like the Great Resignation, but it is laced with the intention of bringing light to the darkness for healing.

3

Let's go back to the winter of 2021, December 10th to be exact. I had a doctor's appointment with my Primary Care Provider that morning. She was, is, the doctor who has kept me alive for many years. She fought for me to find answers and got me in to see every specialist imaginable in order to get me down to Mayo Clinic in Minnesota because she knew, somehow, there would be the place we would find the answers.

She was right. I feel as though I owe her my life. A vast debt one can never repay, but one I know she wouldn't agree with as it is "her job" to do all she did for me. No, Dr. Binning is most certainly not that kind of doctor. The one who takes all the credit herself, though she should. She is like a rare bird you can hardly ever find, but all the books talk about how beautiful it is. There simply aren't enough doctors in the world like her.

Okay, so now that I have sung her praises (not for the first time, nor the last I am certain) – and no, I am not just kissing her ass – let's talk about the discussion we had during my "catch up" appointment. We were talking about the changes I had made in my life. The ways I had grown, and the way my health had made a sudden and dramatic turnaround, leaving me healthy.

GAH!

That word is so foreign to me, and yet here I sit saying that I am it . . . I truly never thought I would see the day when I would be able to say, "I AM HEALTHY" and not have it mean "for now," or "today."

Seriously, that is how sick I was. I may not have had terminal cancer, but my diagnosis was permanent, nearly killed me multiple times, and made my life and the interactions with specific people (George and Wendy) absolutely fraught with stress and anxiety.

You know something I simply will never understand?

Why the hell other people feel the need to diminish someone who is chronically ill as though they are better than them. Why the hell we think "being healthy" is equivalent to "being superior" and so we treat those who are sick as though they are society's pariahs.

For fuck's sake, if you have ever been sick for longer than three days and you know that feeling of wishing life would get back to normal while wondering if it will ever be the same as it was before, TRY FUCKING LIVING THAT WAY FOR MOST OF YOUR ADULT LIFE.

I am the epitome of a walking miracle these days. I get that. I know it is the truth. I take it in stride and choose not to flaunt it.

Why not?

1. I have no earthly idea how this happened. I don't know how I suddenly became the picture of health.

2. I know what it is like to be on the other side, and I have a really bad habit of "waiting for the other shoe to drop" whenever the Universe hands me a blessing on a silver platter. (This one I blame on the fact it was how most of my life went.)

3. There are still a great many people in the world who are sick and suffering. While it doesn't diminish what I endured, nor does it negate the miracle of which I am now living, it does mean I EMPATHIZE with those people.

Not sympathize. I am not pitying them. I am saying I have been there; I understand, I know the struggle, the pain, and the anger you never show in pictures or to the outside world, but you feel within every part of your being the whole time. I empathize with you all.

That appointment, the subject of how I had changed came up. One of my favorite comments from Dr. Binning that day was, "Your smile reaches your eyes. I have never seen you smile like this before, where it reaches your eyes."

I can say with confidence she was proud of me for my personal growth in that moment. I can say with confidence, she is still proud of me. I can say with confidence, she and I have been through our own kind of battle, our own kind of war and during that appointment we talked about how we made it to the other side. How peace was brought into my life, and I believe to this day that it brings peace to her life.

That was the other comment she made to me. She said, "It isn't often I allow a patient to take up rental space in my mind and heart, but you definitely have your own space in both."

Smiling from ear to ear I responded with, "Well, you can take me out of your worry room now."

And she did.

Before that beautiful exchange, we had another. Perhaps I am jumping back to this place because it is what I need to hear. Perhaps it is because it is what you need to hear.

Considering I am not convinced that all this writing isn't simply shit that is just taking up space on my OneDrive and giving me a daily outlet to pour shit out of my mind and heart so I can function without the crushing stress of "What the fuckery is this now?" continuing to plague me, who knows. Regardless of the reasoning for it, let's go back a little bit into this appointment.

Dr. Binning asked me what it was I changed.

What did I do?

How did I do it?

What do I think changed me?

My answer, and I did not hesitate for a moment on it, "I stopped being a victim."

WHAM! BAM! THANK YOU, MA'AM!

Yes, I said it. That thing all spiritual teachers say. The thing you hate hearing when you don't want to believe you are in the victim mindset. The argument you make because you *are* a victim.

You know what, I was a victim too, but that doesn't mean I have to think like one. It doesn't mean I have to be one again and again in my life. No, not me, I choose a different way of thinking and being.

Dr. Binning responded with, "I noticed that. When the kids started talking about what they suffered and you saw them showing the same patterns of behaviors as you once did, I watched you change. You shifted into a fighter and an advocate so fast. It was amazing to see. And now look at you!"

Okay guys, so I am of course paraphrasing a lot of what she said, mostly because there were names that I cannot disclose, and situations in which the stories are not mine to tell, and I know someday my children will begin to tell their own stories. Hell, my daughter Izzie is already telling her stories to people in competitive speech.

She's doing a speech to persuade on how the United States needs to change the Child Protective Services department so that children are heard over the voice of their abusers, abusers are held accountable, and have to go through courses, and therapy, and prove a genuine change so they can be reunited with their children in a healthy environment.

Talk about making lemonade from a basket full of lemons. I have never been so proud of that girl as I am when she speaks her truth into the world while still loving her father so incredibly much. We could all learn a lot about the nature of unconditional love from her, but alas, she is only thirteen, so it is for me to share now and her to share later.

I became a fighter. I became an advocate. There is extraordinarily little I would allow myself to fight for when it came to me years ago. When it was about protecting my children, you had better bet I would be the first one holding a picket sign on the front lawn of the courthouse screaming for a change.

It is the love of being a mother to such amazing tiny humans that made me realize I was doing absolutely zero justice to myself and my children by allowing my worth and sense of self to be dictated by other people.

Ah the dreaded true Achilles heel of mine. Caving to other people's beliefs and opinions of me and my worth. Fuck them all, I decide what I am worth now. Maybe I am here to do what others have done but do it in my own, unique butterfly unicorn way – teach you how to not give a fuck about the opinions of others.

Maybe I am here to just get all this shit out of my head so I don't have to relive it anymore, and I can honestly just walk away having washed my hands clean of all the shit and bridges I had to burn on my spiritual journey.

Fuck, maybe I am here because mother nature wanted to use a slushy, flooded, piles-of-wet-dog-poop nature trail to teach me about taking wrong turns, getting lost, and the way that things once found aren't as grand as they are the second time around.

We build up this spiritual journey in our minds because we need to believe in something bigger than ourselves, and from my personal experiences, the church has really laid bare the destruction of faith as it was for centuries with their fearmongering and lies.

BRING ON THE PITCHFORKS!

I can take it.

There are far too many people in the world enduring religious deconstruction from the damage and the lies for me to give a flying fuck what the church or religious fanatics have to say about my take on things. If I can see eye to eye on faith with my mother, a devout Lutheran, then I think I can handle anything anyone throws my way on it.

You keep your faith, sweetheart, and I will stand firm in my own personal truths. We can agree to disagree, just don't diminish me and I won't return the fucking favor.

That was a bit harsh, perhaps, but I have had my fill of people telling me how I should believe in myself or things in the world. I have had my fill of people who believe they know me and know what is best for me, when in reality these are people who want what is right for them that they are able to take from me.

Do you recognize what it is that I am saying? Are you experiencing people doing this same thing? Fuck them. Walk away from them. If you love them, genuinely love them, nothing toxic about the love shared, then open your mouth, and let your truth ring out from your beautiful throat chakra.

-4-

Alright, so we have established that in the beginning of December of 2021, I figured out that I wasn't willing to continue being a victim of others, nor of my own thoughts and feelings. Fuck that life, I don't want it and don't need it being a part of my life going forward anymore.

Want to know my personal truth about you?

You don't need to be a victim either.

In fact, my truth is we aren't meant for that life at all, and it is within all of our own power to change that completely.

Here's something I have learned about myself; I am a fucking gem. I am someone people want to know. In the past, I found I was someone people wanted to use. And that fact is why I have become deeply selective over who I allow into my world.

It takes trial and error to learn lessons in life a lot of the time. This was definitely one of my harshest trial and error life lessons. It was literally two and a half weeks, perhaps three weeks later when the person I viewed as my "gay best friend" let his true colors shine.

One reason why I feel like the spiritual community seriously needs a wakeup call is centered around the lesson I learned when I trusted a person's words over my own intuition. Despite his verbal attacks on me, the anger and rage that welled within me, called for me to make a choice. Either step forward, be the bigger person, and simply cut ties as cleanly as possible or choose to call him every insult floating around my rage filled mind.

Why would I diminish who I am in order to lower myself to another person's standards?

Why would you?

A couple weeks after I had that appointment, my former friend decided I was being selfish for taking care of myself. I went on an inner healing journey as Venus went into Retrograde. I heard what my guides were calling me to evaluate within. I was being called to do a deeper healing surrounding my past, my traumas, and my wounds internally.

Everyone who has done this journey will tell you the ultimate truth: HEALING IS NOT LINEAR. We don't fully heal from something the first time, nor the second time, nor the third. We have to learn it, heal it, speak of it, get it out of us, and then integrate it.

Every one of those steps requires a new healing journey. So when my former friend wanted to know what it was I had "left" to heal and I said my entire life, I was being selfish to him.

Why?

Because his dog died.

Because he wanted free reiki sessions.

Because he wanted to utilize my gifts, drain my energy, and take for himself so he would feel better without wondering what it was doing to me.

According to him, I was selfish, and cruel, and abandoned him at the time of his need without a thought or care.

What he didn't know was I cried.

I mourned.

I had to heal from it.

Why?

Because I fucking love hard and love deep. When I cut you out of my life, it hits and break my heart. Then you know what I have to do? FUCKING HEAL AGAIN! Jesus H!

Do you think this is fun?

Do you think at this point the spiritual journey is one that is the greatest flowery-rainbow-sparkles lifestyle?

STOP FUCKING THINKING THAT WAY!

Spiritual teachers tell you the willy-nilly frilly shit. They tell you thoughts create your reality, and if you think yourself out of your negativity, your life will suddenly get better. The Secret is one of the worst offenders.

Now, don't get me wrong, it works for some. They are ones whose souls signed up for it to be like a magic wand in their lives. I have the feeling though, that time is coming to an end. All those who had sudden success from bullshit peddling are about to fall. Maybe that is my deep desire for justice. Maybe I am thinking a new reality into existence.

Maybe, just maybe, I am telling you a prophecy right now. Something I have seen for months. Something I have known for months, which means it is coming. Oh boy, is it ever.

I am fucking ready for it too. Do you know how many people peddle complete bullshit in the spiritual community?

I am in no way saying the entirety of the spiritual community is this way. I could list a number of teachers, Tarot readers, and influencers who are absolutely real about what they tell people. They talk about the same kind of things I am saying right here to you.

No I am not trying to live up to them, I am living up to myself, but if you are someone who has a lot of doubt and challenges others, then real talk, it is time to start listening to yourself.

The ones I am truly talking about are those who use fear to get what they want from others. The ones who talk about their painful experiences and then make you pay an exorbitant sum of money in order to learn their secret way of being.

As though they have all the hidden secrets of the world, and you cannot discover them on your own. Those are the ones I see coming to find their secrets aren't helping others, because they are meant to help them.

There is a vast difference between telling your story in the hopes of inspiring people to live more true to themselves and being no different than the long line of people throughout history hoarding truths to maintain power. Power is not meant to be wielded over others; it is meant to be a platform of spreading truth of fucking equality.

When did we fucking forget this fact?

Can you tell I get pissy when there are people who want to do nothing more or less than diminish others, all the while doing absolutely NOTHING of worth during their day. I know I am being judgmental right now, but you want to know what, I have dealt with too many people who are spiritually bypassing, making false promises, and then take money from others by giving them false hope.

Fuck them!

Fuck that!

Fuck it all!

Now, I am going to give you a caveat to all of this. I am telling you the spiritual journey is not all happy times, but that does not mean I am in any way trying to dissuade you from embarking upon this path. It is the path you are already on. Some of you know this, some of you are finding it out, and an even greater number of you are still sleeping to this fact.

We are all on a spiritual journey. It looks different for each and every one of us, just as we are all different from every other person in the world right now. We are wearing these bodies, our personalities/egos are the only ones we get to be in the way we are in this life, but our souls are eternal. Every soul is on a journey, which means every one of us is on a spiritual journey.

I do not separate the spiritual journey from the journey of life. Weird though it may be, I don't think that notion of separation needs to be in existence, nor do I think any separation needs to be in existence. All these constructs we create to make things one way or the other without realizing the middle path. The one that incorporates all possibilities and potentialities. The bridge. The tightrope we walk connecting the chasm of one thing and another, bravely standing in the middle, always working to maintain the balance.

Life, love, spirituality, they are all one in the same when we talk about journeys, paths, purposes. The end point for everything is always love. We go about it in different ways, but the end point, the trajectory is always love.

-5-

You know, I thought that we would see a decrease of profanity, but apparently this isn't the time for it quite yet. It will come, or it won't. Kind of like this will be published, or it won't.

Does it matter one way or the other?

No.

Why?

Because this is giving my anger, my indignation, my sense of deep injustice floating around in a chaotic, nonsensical world a place to land, and a place to play. Gets this shit out of my fucking head and onto paper.

This is the epitome of long overdue purging. I, for one, am super curious to see just what level of shit I have been holding in and not speaking about, because I bet it is even more than I am fully aware of.

Welcome to how purging works. You come to the realization you are holding too much shit inside of you. You can't just brain dump and verbally assault someone else through word vomit. No, that will not do. So you find a way to get it out.

Some people use a voice diary. Some people use videos. Some, like me, have so many journals it is outrageous to own this amount of paper, but I am holding on to them like they are trees and I need oxygen.

Why would I hold onto pages and pages of negativity?

Why should you?

And believe me you should.

The best reason why that I can give you is that burning it or destroying it is bullshit. It doesn't just magically remove something when you haven't healed it and haven't integrated a new truth fully. It is a waste of an experiment. So what I do is hold on to them, and when I feel it is time to go back and review, I go back and review. See the progress made. Take the win to the fucking bank.

Everyone is going to peddle their own opinion upon you for what exactly it is that you should do. Some will tell you to burn letters and pages of negativity. Some will tell you to throw out and clear the clutter of the years of your life. I told you to hold onto them so you can review and see your progress right in front of you.

We all have our ways of doing this journey, of healing, of clearing our mental clutter. We all have our own ways of cleansing ourselves from what came before. No one wants toxicity to linger. No one wants to be inundated with stagnant, go nowhere energy. Me, I had so much of my own wisdom and knowledge challenged, I developed my method of holding onto things so that I had reference points to return to when needed.

You may choose to do it differently. I won't lie. I have thrown things away, I have burned pieces of paper with intentions, goals, and memories written on them. Those were the times I knew without a doubt that I was absolutely, unequivocally finished with that specific lesson. Only when I was certain the lesson was learned thoroughly and integrated fully would I allow for the potential for the lesson supplements to be removed.

I admit, right here and now, I have a perfectionist nature. I don't know whether it is from my life, or it is part of my very soul. I know I have to fight it from time to time lest it hold me back, but when it comes to my healing and personal/soul growth, I do not allow for anything more or less than what I view to be perfect.

We have now successfully established just how fun this journey can be, I mean come on, we are having fun here right? I know I at least am. But this is a section called Timeline Jumping, so let's make some leaps through time so that you can get a feel for what it is that I am going to talk to you all about when it comes to the nitty gritty spiritual healing and growth journey that people just don't seem to want to discuss in normal conversation.

2011 – Kundalini Awakening

Pure unadulterated hell in my day-to-day life. There was no singular person who could tell me I wasn't absolutely certifiably insane. In fact, George did his absolute best to make me feel and believe I was actually crazy AF.

Not only did he utilize the worst forms of gaslighting and manipulation during the course of my Kundalini awakening, effectively removing the beautiful memories I could have of that time, he also was drugging me with Propranolol. George was well aware of a nifty little quirk of my body with medications that impact the blood brain barrier.

Nice guy, right?

Yeah well, at the time and for many years I loved him. One of the hardest truth pills I have had to swallow is in openly admitting the fact that I really did love George. It was my mother who put it into perspective for me.

You just don't allow for these things to continue, you don't kick your spouse out without knowing if they will ever come back, welcome them back without knowing if it will be better, risking your children's mental health, if you do not absolutely love a person. If I am completely honest with you all, which is what I am here for, I should have learned this lesson before I allowed George back in my home, but I didn't.

I cannot look back with regrets nor sorrow. Sometimes I do look back and see nothing but pain and anger. Even those don't last because I think about what I gained from the marriage.

I walked away with two amazing children from that time.

I walked away with a firmer sense of what I will and will not ever again endure within a relationship (and that is across the board relationships – if you try to manipulate or use me, if you are narcissistic, well, I have a door, and you will be the exception to the "Open Door" policy that I hold in my life).

We don't always end where we thought we would, sometimes it isn't even where we wanted to be, but it is always exactly what we need. That isn't an easy thing to accept in the midst of the pain and anguish of a broken marriage and family. I always hated when people would say, "Everything happens for a reason," and now it has become one of my soothing mantras when shit hits the fan. Isn't that just a twist of fate? Let's take a quick look at some of the everything that happened for whatever reason.

2015 – Did someone say life Overhaul?!

George and I finally split up, and my spiral down into depression, suicide, self-harm in new and inventive ways, and an internal triggering tumble down of activations within me began. This also happened to be the year I met my husband, though we wouldn't begin dating for another year, and wouldn't be married for another three.

I can be petty on this topic, and well sometimes we have to embrace the sheer ridiculous nature of the life and things we have kept ourselves silent on – not to mention as of right now, this is a bitch fest of purging for all the shit that I never talk about because I am always, for whatever fucked up reason, embracing the act of "being the mother fucking bigger person."

If you have ever been the bigger person continually, I know you definitely get where I am coming from. As I am working through the edits of this book, I am realizing how much built-up anger, resentment, and bitterness I have had over the years. I am also noticing a wicked pattern of thoughts which means we need to take a tangent break and discuss this.

When I do my personal and shadow work journaling this is the part I would put an asterisk midway through a thought or at the end of a thought to add an "of note" blurb. It is my way of calling myself out. How about we do that here?

---

*Of note: As I am editing and working through the aftermath of this level of purging, and the emotional letdown that came after completing the first round of this, I am picking up a new thought process of which I was not earlier aware.

I am noticing the parts of what I have written that make me feel as though I need to become defensive about what I have said. The way I am fearful of how others will perceive and judge me, and the multitude of arguments from the spiritual community I could potentially hear about my vibration, worthiness of being a spiritual teacher, and the fact all I am doing is low-vibrational bitching.

It's like the Insecurity Fairy (which if anyone wants to know what this lovely fairy is all about, check out my second book, *And What If...*) is flitting all around whispering in my ear continually. Now I can't help but think about why it is I write my "of notes" as though I would ever present my deep darks to the world and wondering if my writing style has become all about writing for other people.

Am I always going to be the one that doesn't do anything specifically for myself? I should probably get off this tangent before I end up going in a mental spiral of questioning myself and then scrapping this whole thing and the whole purpose of this journey and this story really will be lost in the ethers of my worries and people pleasing tendencies. CAN I RIP IT OUT OF ME YET?

"Of notes," are great opportunities to be completely honest with yourself. They are my design which came into being through the "sidenotes" my husband and I use when we are texting and talking to each other, and there is an off-topic thing that just pops into our heads.

These catch your own mind's spiral thinking patterns off guard, and you don't really have the time to cover it up. It's the surprise ambush to stop the negativity in its tracks and bring it into form on the page in front of you, keeping it from becoming a hum of self-sabotage in the background of your own mind.

So why was 2015 such a pivotal point? Though I will get into it in more detail, there is the small factor of George's infidelity with the woman who pretended to be my friend, sent me nude pictures of herself, slept with his little brother first, and of course got caught posting inappropriate pictures online, an act quite unbecoming for a schoolteacher in a small town.

She promptly accused someone of revenge porn (and yes, I called her out to the person that she accused; it was petty, but I was destroyed by the fact these two people had effectively made a unilateral decision to destroy the life, family, and love I had held onto with a death grip of delusions – never said I was the smartest during this time).

All these points of indignation I have felt on and off over the years boil down to a truth needing to be let go of: I based my worth on the relationship I was in.

I felt completely unworthy of love. How could he choose her over me? How could he choose someone who was so duplicitous and manipulative over me? Yet, I had to face the fact I was not much better of a person before.

I had to face my own inner demons and wrong choices to see that I too was contributory to this all falling apart. I wasn't a victim, but it became easier to feel that way rather than see it as the opportunity it was to become my full self finally.

There is also the fact that George abandoning me and our children, cutting us off financially, and deciding his money was better spent on a trip to the Bahamas to get engaged to a woman he had known in person for two weeks, effectively led to me and our children being evicted.

---

*Of note:** As I am once more working through edits, I am finding my mind doing something different than normal. Instead of seeing all the things I am sharing as being bitching and whining, I am seeing all the things I have overcome.

Here's the thing, I am being as candid as I am through this writing process, and in bringing this book to the world because I have not found another person who would be willing to allow someone else into their inner world enough to not feel alone. I also know I have a tendency to break myself down all the while building others up.

This is something I have fought with for years, but through something as cathartic as embracing a passion I have for writing and sharing with others, showing them the things they struggle to see within themselves, I too find healing. This is symbiosis. This is collaboration on a grand scale. This is how we build each other up while we are broken down. We reach out a hand, no matter if we are at the top or the bottom, and we pull.

It is in these moments, I feel deep gratitude for all I have endured, the people who have challenged me, those who have taught me valuable lessons, and the ones who have been unknown support along the way. I find myself in this moment in awe of myself.

I share this "of note" with you all because this is too another part of this healing journey. It may not all be easy, but there are moments where the sun does break through the clouds. Embrace those moments more fully than you embrace the trials. For it is the revelations of light that bring you through the hardest times, even if you struggle with recall in the moment. They are always there within you.

Fear distorts possibility and hope, every single time. In that time, there was nothing but fear coursing through my being, day in and out. Building up, pressurizing my inner world, getting me prepared for what was to come. I simply couldn't see it hidden behind the distortion.

Thank fucking god my mom had the fiscal resources to help me out. Not everyone has that situation available, and we were blessed beyond belief to have love and support then and now.

I also became a raging alcoholic, fell in love with my best friend, and was relearning how to be a human being when all I knew myself as was a wife and mother lacking worth.

I had given up every other aspect of my being to do whatever it was George needed from me or the children needed of me. My drinking raged out of control in the start of the divorce proceedings.

If it were not for David telling me point blank I needed to quit, or he couldn't be around me, I realized how widely I was spreading my pain around everywhere.

It was a big fucking transition year that feels like it is just starting to taper down, and it is 2022 as I am writing this.

2016 – Karmic Saturn Pattern! AH!

My fucking Saturn return. Did I realize at the time that is what was going on? Fuck no. Do I see now just what a train wreck, bulldozer moment, or year/couple of years this astrological event really was? Yep.

I lost a uterus, an ovary, my tonsils, cancer, my sense of self, one dream job, two dream jobs, my sense of dignity, my ability to have children, and so much more. I lost my health. I lost my heart-centered nature. I lost many friends. I lost my ability to trust. I lost my immune system.

That is a lot of shit to lose during a Saturn return. Again, it has been 6 years since the official transits to the place of Saturn in my birth chart, and I am still working through the magnitude of changes it wrought in my life.

I won't lie, I still don't have a full grasp on just what it was that Saturn brought back into my life, what was activated within, and how it is going to continue to play out. Saturn is an interesting planet, one I feel a deep love and respect for, though it was not always like this.

Perception of things and events shape our impression of ourselves and the world. This is my personal truth; it is one of the only ones that never seems to change. I won't go completely into what Saturn is, what the return of Saturn means, for that is not the point of this book.

All there is to take away from this time, for me and for you, is there were forces beyond my current awareness in 2016 impacting me and my life in deep, profound ways. I would be willing to bet you could discover similar insights if you have gone through a Saturn return as well.

Some are more profound than others, some even are blessed to have good things rush in from Saturn's return, but we all experience a massive change of situations and life.

2019 – Brink of death.

Okay, so I am skimming over a few years' time. They were a hazy mess of wine, tears, insecurities, and me putting people through hell while being in a state of hell. We will discuss it when we jump around here and there, but for the most part those times were just setting up for the year we moved into the house I am currently living in.

When I moved into this house, I began engaging in a series of behaviors and obsessions with certain notions not a single person could have prepared me for. Here's the thing, there are Ley Lines running through the earth.

These are like energetic boundaries, tied to specific places, carrying a specific energy signature. I moved houses and moved onto a new ley line. One that is tied to Ancient Egypt, which I just so happen to have a few (to say the least) past life connections to. Upon beginning to interact with the energy, my life took a fuck of a turn.

Like a serious fucking overhaul of bullshit. I almost died, on several occasions. I had liver failure, kidney's shutting down, and a brain tumor (which I will admit there was no evidence, and we will talk about it. It just so happens to be an important lesson about how your intuition will tell you the ultimate truth of yourself, and your body, and your life, and no one will ever dissuade you from that).

That is just the tip of the iceberg. There were also the minimal sleeping nights, the random mental and emotional purging moments which nearly destroyed my sense of self and safety within who I am and made me take a long hard look in the mirror.

2020 – Pandemic. Lock down. Court. Hell.

Realizations up the wazoo. And dealing with actually seeing George and his manipulation and abuse in black and white in front of me. For real though, this was a year of losses, battles, wins, and realizations. It was when I finally threw caution to the wind and said, bring on my psychic gifts only to follow up less than ten minutes later with sheer panic and saying "too much! It is too much! Make it stop! FUCK!!!!"

In October of 2020, I was in the midst of a nasty custody battle, facing being held in contempt of court for violating the agreement between George and me, and dealing with the pinnacle moment of health-related fears. I finally took the steps in mid-October to becoming sober, a sobriety I maintain to this day.

Pouring out all the alcohol in my home after being held in contempt of court without incurring any punishment, for the judge found the reasoning to be justified, I knew without a doubt a change of epic magnitude needed to happen in my life. I began having migraines once more. These were not infrequent, nor were they tied to withdrawal symptoms.

They were accompanied by a change in my vision that resulted in eye doctor appointments confirming I had suddenly, at the age of 33, developed an astigmatism. I was told this was highly unusual.

Then the apathy and aphasia set in. Suddenly I was sitting in my kitchen trying to say the word refrigerator, and I no longer had the word in my vocabulary. After that was the constant vertigo. I was on a ship, buffeted by waves, day in and day out.

There were many times I would have to ask if I was swaying or if it was the room moving. Most of the time it was not me engaging in the motion. Back to Dr. Binning I went!

There was a concern on her face I had never before seen, and an insurance based red-tape complication preventing her from being able to order the imaging studies she wanted.

There is a look, an awfully specific look, doctors get when there is a strong suspicion of a serious problem. It was one I had seen before, shortly before being sent to Oncology to schedule a bone marrow biopsy.

There it was again.

Dr. Binning's face is never where I would want to see it either. I knew from one singular look; I was barking up the right tree in my thought processes.

Referrals were put in for me to go to see a Neurologist. More red tape. It was required for me to see a Nurse Practitioner to determine if I was worthy to see a Neurologist. The appointment wasn't possible for another two months.

Dr. Binning called the office to attempt to facilitate reasoning, but she was restricted and limited by both the insurance and the hospital policies. The Nurse Practitioner called me, and we spoke over the phone. She consulted with a Neurologist.

This is when the phone calls attempting to convince me to go immediately to the Emergency Room started. Do not pass Go, do not collect $200.

"Go get an emergent MRI. Immediately."

Days of these phone calls. During a pandemic. While I had no immune system and the halls were lined with COVID-19 patients, many of whom did not walk out of the hospital. I was not willing to risk it. I had children. I had a family. I could not justify that risk.

There had to be another way. There I was, feeling as though modern medicine had finally, completely failed me. Fear coursing, coursing, coursing through me all the time. It was 9 pm on a Thursday night. I had cleaned my kitchen, cup of coffee in hand, when I broke down.

"This cannot be it. I cannot have a brain tumor and have to choose between letting it go or risk getting a deadly virus to check it out. I just realized how much of myself I was sacrificing! I just realized how many hopes and dreams I have! This cannot be the end of my life when I am just starting to live finally!"

The next morning I went into research mode. I found out about an experimental treatment using sound wave caps for brain tumor patients. This led me on a discovery journey for myself.

I found Solfeggio Frequencies, Binaural Beats, the Wim Hof Method, and Rife Frequencies. It was the first time I set an intention with the Universe. I was going to use these techniques and I would heal myself. It would work. There was no doubt, there was only one option: health.

Within a month everything aside from the astigmatism had healed. And when I say everything, I do mean, everything. I found out later I had opened up something within me, a natural healer part of me I never knew existed. I learned Reiki. I learned about everything I could possibly get my hands on. I wasn't sick anymore. I didn't understand it at all.

Sometimes the intentions we set when we don't know we are setting intentions, working with the Law of Attraction, are the most powerful. I didn't know about manifestation back then, but it is what I believe I was gifted with. I was experiencing a miracle for the seemingly first time. All the while, I began the journey which brought me here.

Everyone is going to remember 2020 as the year of COVID-19, the year the world was locked down. It was my year of miracles and destruction, for I have learned, or at least begun to believe, you cannot have one without the other – and on that note let's move to the fuckery that was 2021.

2021 – FUCK, FUCK, FUCKETY FUCK!

Seriously. That is what the year was. I became a Reiki Grand Master, published two books, experienced three days' worth of stigmata, was brain washed, met awesome people, met some of the worst people, learned to see behind the veil of most of the spiritualists out toting their bullshit in the world, and oh yeah, the fucking stigmata shit.

Let's also mention the fact that I began having some seriously fucked prophetic visions – which began to come true within days of me having them. They continued right through fucking Putin, the war in Ukraine, and the Black Swan event of the Russian economy. What a fucking year it was.

I have written and edited this book several times now, and every time I come back to the "synopsis" portion of 2021, I know there is much I am leaving out. Much of this year is contained in the following pages and lessons, but what I want to talk about is numerology here.

In numerology, we consider the energy of numbers. The unique signature numbers carry in the world, and how we interact with these numbers in our lives. I do not think I would be off-the-mark to say 2021 changed the world in many ways. It changed my world in more ways than I can count. It used to be something I would reflect on, but the sheer magnitude of what happened throughout the year has on multiple occasions left me feeling overwhelmed, my head spinning in circles.

2021 = 2+0+2+1=5. 2021 was a 5 energetic year. This is the energy of change. The energy of adventure, fluctuations, upheaval, and order being found within disorder. There are many different interpretations of numerical energy, some following Pythagorean Numerology, some favoring Chaldean Numerology, some following symbolism from the Tarot. For me I combine a lot of these theories together with my own personal interactions with the numbers themselves.

It was a 5 year, 2021. And my year was encompassed by this energy in everything. All the changes, all the different adventures, and not a single one of those involved me leaving my home. Strangely enough, it was as 2021 was coming to a close, I found myself feeling strongly as though I had traversed not only the globe, but through time, forward and back, and I had finally found myself home. Home in my body. Home in my mind. Home in my life.

The level of relief I felt from this return, I cannot explain. It was when I came back home to myself, all of what I am writing about began to fall into place within my mind, clearing clutter, and the emotional purging came in. All to prepare me for the upcoming energy of 2022, a 6 year. A year of change followed by a year of harmony, balance, and unconditional love. A year of return.

2021 was the year everything changed so consistently, I was not able to find firm footing. I found myself pulled in many directions, shifting from one dream to another. Running from my hopes and desires and dreams to do what was expected of me. Falling into old patterns and learning to break free of those very patterns of being. It was a year in which I had no other option but to face down all the inner demons for it was time to usher in peace and truth fully into my life.

-6-

This leads us to right now. 2022. It's Aries season! Okay, so this year's Aries' season has me seriously excited. Pisces season ran a train through my mental and emotional health. You know what? If it weren't for that, I would not be sitting here writing this because it definitely started in fucking Pisces season. I began doing this thing in 2022, in fact I started it around February.

I decided that I was going to forego tracking time based on the Gregorian calendar and become more energetically based in my emotions and time frames of reference. Sure there are still 24 hours in the day, and all that fun stuff, but it isn't about the first of any month for me anymore, no it is when the zodiac seasons change.

It is all about the cycles of the moon, the energies in the cosmos and where it is that I am living my best self in any given moment in time. I am trying to return to the days of the stars being the guides, and the heavens and their bodies being my teachers.

This way of living means I am beginning to understand which of the zodiac seasons really impact me the greatest, and how it interacts with my natal chart. Astrology is a love of mine. It is a deep love, a passionate embrace, and with every deep and passionate love, there is a high risk of being burnt.

Astrology can't really be burned from me, but fuck does it pack a punch. We will talk more about that as we go. I have the feeling that whether this becomes anything more than just the ramblings of my mind, in a sort of "Morning Pages" style from Julia Cameron, that I am not even going to bother to edit this shit. Give it to the world raw and honest.

Spoilers: I am editing. This is one of my insecurity blocks. If I half-ass, half-commit, then if I fail, I can blame myself and beat myself up forever. Sometimes, realizing how much I sabotage myself is illuminating. Other times, I want to have a firm talk with myself and tell myself to knock this shit off.

Yeah, sure I can call myself lazy and whatever. I don't want to edit it, I don't want to go down the rabbit hole of bullshit with trying to get an agent, get published, whatever. But as Reid Tracy likes to say, if you are writing for your heart and your art, do it your way and fuck the system. I am paraphrasing, a lot. He is far more eloquent than that, but well, this is not a book of eloquence.

This is a book of raw reality.

Fuck.

Shall we move on?

---

*Of note: Did you see how I justified my own shadows? Did you see how I used a logical argument to justify illogic? Splendid! I saw it too. This is important for me to see, but it is also important for you to understand about yourself as well. It isn't always the easiest thing to accept we do this to ourselves.

Acceptance is something coming after awareness. So here we are becoming aware together. Self-sabotage is a tricky little bitch to find and overcome. The second you see it, it changes. For this reason, using a tool like the "Of notes" keeps you brutally honest with yourself on this journey as well. I will always say, and my family can vouch for this, "Honesty is the best policy."

As a mother, I have house rules. The number one rule in my house is "Always tell the truth." You will never get in trouble for being honest but lies destroy so much.

Any empath will tell you, we are literally walking, talking lie detectors. It makes dishonesty from the ones you love a major challenge to overcome. Dishonesty with myself, well, that is no longer an option for me.

In order to be who I truly am, to do the things I want in the world, I have to be completely transparent with myself. I am my own worst enemy. I know this. I am also my biggest supporter. It is about honesty and balance.

I find myself coming to the end of this section on Timeline Jumping and realizing you may be wondering what the bigger reasoning for what all of this was beyond just talking to you about the things that have happened and making allusions to subjects to come.

The reason I set all this up ties back to my first book *Chemistry with Kismet,* and also is tied to a principle of shamanism: Inventory. What is the very last thing anyone wants to do after surviving hell and high water? Go back over it.

No one wants to review things in their life, because isn't that considered wallowing in pity and engaging in self-deprecation? No, no it isn't. It is about the energy you bring to going back over the things from your past. It is about becoming an observer, as though you are Peter Pan floating over the scenes of your past, watching without engaging in it.

When you do this, you give yourself the space between who you were and who you are, what happened then and the reality of your life now. Doing these timeline jumps to take inventory of the moments that have challenged you, the times you have overcome, and the hardships you have overcome bring to you a different image of who you truly are in the midst of the momentary struggles.

Imagine if we could see all situations like this in the moment? There is someone demeaning you, and you are able to see it from a higher perspective, knowing fully the person is projecting, and there is no need or good done to respond. You remain calm, grounded, and centered. And now you have managed to circumvent the struggle internally from the past.

This is why we timeline jump. This is why we purge. This is why we speak about these times, these struggles, these hardships. So we are able to transcend the fuck out of each and every one of them.

Where Do We Go from Here

Am I supposed to have the answers to your burning questions on spirituality? I suppose being a Spiritual Life Coach, a Shadow Work Coach, and well, a fucking psychic. I should have some sort of answers for you. I don't know a single one of them are what you want to hear.

Let's cover the things I know you don't want to hear, the pieces that you should swallow or burn the fuck out of this book and walk the fuck away. Choice is totally yours.

#1 –

The Healing game we talk about, yeah, it is sugar coated as fuck. All those secrets you are holding deep within yourself. The things you swore you would take to the grave? No you won't. Not if you are *serious* about actually healing. Sure you can keep them, hold them in, never speak out about them, never speak your truth.

You won't grow. You may learn how to cheat the system with fear-based living and feeding off of others' fears to do so.

Hell, it seems to be what everyone does, but that won't ever absolve your soul.

Absolution isn't like they teach in religion. Absolution is all about freedom. It is about lightening the load of what you carry with you from day to day. It is about finding your inner truth, your way forward, and embracing your life here. It isn't about getting out of going to hell, it isn't about getting into heaven.

Soul absolution is about rising above the melee, letting in more truth, and fighting for a better way forward in the world for you, your children, and humanity as a whole.

If it were as easy as dropping money in the offering plate once a week, and taking a shot of wine to wash down the wafer, cleansing you of all the bullshit you did the week prior, don't you think we all would be living the lives we are meant to?

#2 –

Spiritual bypassing, when you are working with me, talking to me, engaging in a friendship, mentorship, or any sort of professional or personal relationship with me, is ABSOLUTELY NOT OKAY. Given the opportunity I would gladly tell you who I have seen out there in the spiritual community doing this "we don't spiritually bypass here" and then following it up with a series of videos or teachings that are LITERAL SPIRITUAL BYPASSING.

I won't tell you. Once upon a time I did, but that lifestyle kept me in the wrong frame of mind. Once again, without realizing it until later, I was self-sabotaging.

How do I know this?

Am I not just being a judgmental bitch here?

Perhaps, but I have his fun thing called a spiritual alarm system, and it will make me physically ill to be around people who aren't taking care of their soul's growth.

Can you imagine how challenging motherhood has just become on top of the normal everyday shit? Now we add my hypersensitivity on a spiritual level as well. Fucking hell.

You know there are times in which I wonder why my soul is the level of masochist it truly is. What the fuck dude? Like what did you choose to be this way for? I have some cool gifts, but I walked into a local metaphysical shop and could feel the inherent wrongness of the show owner, the way they set everything up, the lingering bad juju of the place, and I nearly hurled on their floor.

Sometimes these things can be uber frustrating when I just want to engage with others, but there aren't others around me I can engage with. Am I bitching? Probably. I am a little bitter about some of this, but I am working my way through it all, right here and now.

Ironically as I am telling you all of this, I have all my spiritual signals that it is okay, I am doing the right thing, and I am free to speak my truth. Weird right? That would be crown tingles, and some sense of an angel next to me. And weirdly enough it feels like my liver is being deeply cleansed.

Do I know what that really means?

Nope.

I just know it is what I am feeling, hearing, and experiencing. Welcome to spiritual gifts (have I said that to you already?).

I have said before, and I will again, our bodies are our greatest form of communication with ourselves. They tell us when we are in the right place and time, and they tell us when we aren't. They tell us what is right for us, and what isn't. Not only that, but our bodies are what hold our souls and our connection to Spirit. This means whatever we feel, we are meant to feel it, sort through it, and learn from it.

Bitterness, it is a normal human emotion. When you learn the ways in which your body communicates with you, you learn how to respond in kind. As you learn this new, natural way of moving through your life, you cease to feel those same "negative" emotions from before. At the very least, if you don't cease to feel them, they cease to overpower you and your responses.

So when I asked if you could clearly see my bitterness about the lessons I had to endure, and talked about working through them, it is a lesson in and of itself for you. Spiritual bypassing is avoiding seeing these things we contain and favoring something called "toxic positivity." This is the "Everything is love and light," mentality. It is glossing over the aspects we find unsavory, choosing to navigate around them, and healing becomes incomplete.

My theory on my soul being a masochist, it was formed from this deep resistance to spiritual bypassing. It was all about the sense of needing a completeness to all I do. Needing to go from start to middle to end and then go through it again to be absolutely certain it took. You can consider it a high standard or consider it an adventure to find your ultimate worth and capability of creating the life you desire. That is a choice solely in your hands.

I choose to move my way through the emotions and bitterness, the struggles and the hardships, so as to have the fullness of the adventure of the human experience.

#3 –

Sometimes I will go off on a tangent. I will lose the seeming thread of what I am talking about, and then magically will end up coming full circle. This requires patience. My brain works differently than most, but there is a method to the madness, a rhyme, and a reason. Even when it seems like there isn't.

So whatever this "work of art" becomes, whether it remains in the annals of my undone or unreleased projects, or if I finish it and decide to offer it for a measly $0.99, or even make it full price, and tout it as the greatest work of literary mastery in the history of the world, it requires a great feat of patience.

Hell, I walked away from this section in order to attempt to get more sleep, this is not the only book I am currently writing right now, and I forgot entirely what the purpose of this section really was all about.

Do I realize now what it is?

Not really.

I think it is just me laying my boundaries down.

Perhaps it will teach you about strength in what is and isn't right for you. God, I really hope so because if I am going to sit down and write this fuck of a situation, this journey down, being brutally honest with you, I would hope that you would get something, anything out of it.

Hopefully more than just the proverbial, "I am never going to go through a spiritual awakening." HA! The second you say that you are literally inviting the Universe to sit at the dinner table with you as it serves you up several heaping helpings of Humble Pie and giggles at your mounting discomfort.

How do I know?

Yep, you guessed it.

I was *never* going to walk a spiritual path.

Alright enough numerical shit. Enough "guidelines for handling a random writing from Monica."

If you have survived this long into this, I don't think you are going anywhere. The self-deprecating me wants to call you a masochist as well, or just assume you are a literary critic ready to throw me to the rest of the wolves, but only after having ripped me to shreds.

Go for it. It won't make your mom or dad love you more than they did before, you won't look tough in front of your friends, and my book will still be out in the world despite your attempts to squelch its message.

Can you imagine if people actually talked to critics like that?

And I do mean any critics.

Some asshole is walking down the street. You are outside in your oversized pajama bottoms you absolutely love. He is walking down the middle of the street randomly carrying a desk lamp, and he has the audacity to make a scathing remark about your pants.

FYI: this is an actual true story. Happened to me back in 2007. I was wearing men's pajama pants. They were the size of JNCO jeans, parachute pants. I probably could have leaped off a ten-story building, and they would have floated me to the ground.

I LOVED those pajama pants.

My dog needed to go to the bathroom, so I was taking him out when this jerk decided he was going to mock my pants and then snicker like a toddler. Seriously, he was definitely in his forties or fifties, and didn't realize I knew he still lived with his mother because he was my neighbor. Yet he believed it was something he was entitled to say, *entitled*.

That word. Critics, judges, assholes, and especially narcissists all suffer from the same illness, I am convinced. It is called Entitlement Ass. As though every time they sit upon a toilet and shit out more of their rainbow golden bars of poop, they become ever more entitled.

I am assuming that's what comes out the back end because the front end is filled with the brown shit spewing from their lips. I am being harsh, but let's be real here, critics live their lives trying to see whose hopes and dreams they are able to crush into powder.

The vast majority of people who have a story to tell, who have an innate gift for communication, find they are perpetually silenced from the fear of what the world will do to them upon sharing. When did we come to a time where we have chosen not to see the sheer strength of someone sharing their darkness and light in the world? When did we get to the point where it became acceptable to pick apart the lives, bodies, thoughts, and emotions of people in the public eye?

Trolls sit behind a computer screen, typing feverishly on their keyboards to make themselves feel self-important. Does it really make them feel better to spread this negativity into the world? No. What it does is make them justify why the world is going to hell, why they shouldn't give two shits about anyone else, and why they have lived their lives ever so wronged by the status quo.

You want to know a secret? If you don't like the status quo, you have to change it. You do that by rising above your narrowed perception, accepting there are differences in all people, and not being a prejudicial asshole about the people who aren't the same as you.

We place boundaries of acceptable behavior for the people around us, and those who don't like boundaries will attack them. They do this because they don't want to be held accountable for their own actions. Do it anyway. Set your boundaries, set your standards, and make sure you are living every single moment true to them.

This is the whole, "be the change you want to see in the world." Don't weigh in on a topic, or a person's situation, if you haven't been invited. Be a kind fucking human being and realize that we all have back stories you don't know and have no right to speak out about.

Ugh, there I go with my own duplicity. I am quite literally weighing in on the lives of others. I am okay with that, because I know, in writing this and giving it to the world, I am opening a door for you to weigh in on it. See, invitation.

Okay, so let's talk about what happened that led me here. I guess I know where we are going to go from here. It is STORY TIME!

We hopped through time, I went off on a tangent of epic proportion to get us to this spot, so let's talk about what really led me to sitting down and needing to get out all of this seeming negativity when really it is just me talking about all the shit in a new way for you all. Hell, I have the feeling, by the time this is all done my throat chakra is going to be shiny and new!

Are you ready?

The Lamb Becomes the Lion

1

Oh, I think I really like the title of this chapter. It just popped into my head as I was "insert page break" on my document. The Lamb, yes that is me, suddenly becomes the Lion. How the hell does one undergo that kind of transition?

It isn't from self-empowerment techniques; I will tell you that. It is from falling to my knees and begging Spirit, my Spirit Guides, my Angels, the Ascended Masters, Archangels, my Ancestors, and the Universe to take the pain out of me, because I reached the "straw that broke the camel's back," finally.

It was the fall of 2021 and I got involved with a program designed to help people live their life purpose as a full-time career. The program itself is not the focal point here, rather it is the community I found myself a part of. The community should have been uplifting. It should have been supportive.

It was a dog-eat-dog, attention-seeking shit fest of people all trying to do the same thing with little to no moderation or actual directed guidance. We all placed trust and a bare minimum of $1000 into what we believed was a secret method to living the life of our dreams.

We all came together; all felt the pulse of projected positivity all influencers use when they speak to crowds. We all were filled with hope and an assurance that here we had found our soul tribe, our community, our support. There was no real sense of community within the community.

I have since left it. But I didn't do so until I had been burned by a group of people I met, save one or two of them. And not before I hurt other people along the way as well.

I wish more or less I were coming here to sing the praises of a program that worked, an investment that paid off, and a group of people who genuinely cared and supported each other.

I wish.

I cannot.

As I said before, I abhor lying. There was a lot of pain in making the decision I did to walk away from the hope I felt, the hope that was dashed.

Here's the thing about when you get hurt. I promise you as you are being hurt, every single time you are hurting someone else. It is the nature of the beast. We aren't designed, or rather aren't conditioned, to accept someone putting up boundaries or doing things that serve themselves first.

Therefore when there is an interaction with a "me first" person, it is the ones with the most hope to lose who, in the beginning, become easy pickings. These are the lambs, being preyed upon by the wolves for they have yet to realize the lion lying in wait within themselves.

There are a great many people peddling programs into the world that have self-serving intentions behind what they do. Don't mistake me here. Of course, a program sponsored by a person or entity should help them. It should also help in the way that is promised. It should also take into account not everyone is formed, nor designed the exact same, thus anything promoted must take into account a multitude of options and methods to serve a large audience.

In the spiritual community, many of these programs and people say, or stake a claim, to being "Lightworkers." Promoting a rosy image of being here to serve when really, they are here to live their lives, make money, and then make false promises.

This is why I don't make promises with my programs. I will tell you what the purpose behind it is. I will tell you what I intend for the results to be. I will tell you how all the programs I build are based solely on my own lessons, and then tell you what changes have occurred in my life. I won't promise you that you will see the same changes.

You are your own person, and the accountability for change lies in your hands, not mine. I am simply the bridge builder, the architect, the one providing the tools and the supplies. I show you how to build what I have already done. Then wish you all the luck in the world, like a mother dropping her child off at the bus stop for the first day of school with a hope comingled with a sense of freedom.

I digress.

Let's get back to this community I found myself in. Now, for the sake of not getting my ass sued, I am following the same lessons I learned when writing *Chemistry with Kismet*, and all the names will be changed.

I will even choose to change some of the actual locations these people lived in because, well if you feel for me through this, I don't want you traversing the world with torches and pitchforks. Just don't be a douche like these people were.

Don't steal another person's personal power.

Don't use someone, and then attack them for walking away from you.

Don't set a standard of operation that involves going behind someone's back and talking shit about them, and then get pissed off when they address you directly, and demand they share screenshots of the messages, so nothing is misconstrued. Yes, I am being vague here on the situation, but try here to focus on the actions. There are three people in a chat, two separate individual chats, and one person discovers there is an energetic mismatch occurring.

All actions taken by the one choosing to walk away becomes a point of attack. A direct conversation is misconstrued as being "behind someone's back," because the person is personally offended by you choosing to extricate yourself from the situation.

They have engaged in this same behavior with a third party, behind your back. When you found out, you requested direct communication, as words are always subject to the telephone game, and you would rather be present to explain yourself rather than deal with this bullshit continually.

Are you getting a sense I am talking about high school? Have you heard the song, "High School Never Ends," by Bowling for Soup? It played in my head on repeat for months.

I found myself, sitting in my bed, crying my eyes out and telling David, "I am so tired of high school bullshit! Why have I had to grow up, and be mature, and be responsible, but everyone else can run around acting like a bunch of fucking teenagers?"

I won't tell you I wasn't having my very own childish moment. Emotions often bring that out in us all. We find ourselves feeling the same way we did at a given point in our lives. In high school, I dealt with a surplus of bullying from adults and classmates, alike. Dealing with people who are out for blood simply because it makes them feel in power over others, it brings out the lonely, pained, and frustrated 16-year-old within me.

I have dealt with some petty fucking people. Selfish as the day is long and self-serving, at least in my perception. And you know what? I learned from them, to prioritize me. I learned to say, "Fuck other people's expectations. I need to heal. I need to be me. I need to follow my heart and live my life how I wish to live it."

So, thank you to the ones who put me through all of those challenging lessons. You taught me to take care of me and my family first, and simultaneously to never treat another person with the same disregard that you treated me.

Now that is what I call self-empowerment.

2

I met this guy. I am a middle-aged, American woman. My whole life I have had one dream (okay so I have had many, but this one is pretty well known across the board), I wanted to have a gay best friend. Yep, I said it. So when I learned that this man was gay it was like a double-triple bonus.

---

*Of note: I have this overwhelming feeling I am setting myself up for attack here. Though it definitely goes against my premise of "I should not defend myself," there is a lot of political controversy in the world we are living with regarding sexuality. I have two children who are bisexual. Two.

I absolutely support freedom to love who you love. It is a frustrating thing to be a writer these days, and attempt to write something that is entirely P.C.

It is about respect.

One cannot make a firm decision, nor form a firm judgement about another without truly knowing them and their background. This is what drives me up the wall. We all pick each other apart for things we lack full awareness of. This is why I keep feeling like people are assholes, even when we aren't meant to be.

Can we not find a way to accept the manner in which someone loves another without feeling we have the right to get involved? It is highly frustrating. Particularly after being the one who has made multiple phone calls to my daughter's school regarding the audacity of the boys in her class bullying her for being out about who she is and who she chooses to love.

While I do not feel as though I should have to justify my word usage, I do feel it is important to make my stance on love crystal clear, as I believe in helping everyone to accept differences and live in harmony.

"Can't force it," quite literally just went through my mind. Thank you guides. They are so wonderful with making sure to remind me, despite how I see the potential for us all to be, the hope I hold onto for others in the world, I cannot change other people. I can only shine a light through my lens of awareness and understanding, holding the intention for it to shine for those who need it.

The fact he fell within the guise of a Human Design Projector, well that was icing on top of the cake. This excitement became problematic for me. I didn't study enough of the Human Design information. When I saw he was an Ego driven decision maker, I should have run for the fucking hills.

Nope, not me.

I dug my heels in, opened my heart, and let myself trust him.

Fucking naivety at its best. David's coworker Jake quite literally told me he wants to have a talk with me about online stranger danger. This coming from a man who plays online RPGs and makes friends with random people left and right. David does the same thing; never runs into the issues I have. A fact I could be bitter about, but it only served to make me question myself.

Why can't that be the case for me?

I discovered it had everything to do with my giving nature. I share my gifts freely with others. At least, I used to. After this friendship, the last in a long line of painful friendships with the same patterns, I learned. People who are operating from an egocentric shadow state, experiencing the kindness and love, the gifts I have, they think me weak, and a tool for their personal use.

That isn't bravado either. I wish it were. I really do. Why? Because then I could just be a selfish, self-serving person like all the other people I have dealt with. They seem to have lived an easier life. In all honesty, this point of view is definitely not accurate.

Glass houses and whatnot. Okay, so their lives aren't necessarily easier, but they don't seem to care about taking advantage of people like me. I have always wondered about these people. It was something I had to learn to stop wondering.

Some people just are how they are. Most have something within still broken from an experience in their life, often from childhood. Questioning the unchangeable (at least through my own actions) is not something I choose to engage in anymore. I don't do futility.

Back to the former gay best friend. He lived across the world from me. Seriously. This is no joke.

We would facetime almost daily, sometimes it would be multiple times in a day. Usually when he would have some sort of crisis. For the most part, I tried to keep my crises to a minimum in communication, but there were times when I consulted him on the approach to George and Wendy. I even asked him for advice on what I could do to help my daughter when the bullying in school continued to amplify.

After the dissolution of the friendship, it was those moments I had gone to him for advice. The calls he made to me with insistence I answer, despite me not wanting to share my struggles openly, those were the moments he attacked when I could no longer engage in the toxic, one-way friendship. He threw out a comment about not mentioning the "rollercoaster of a life," after I cut him out of my life. Remember when I said, when you are hurting, you hurt others. Nature of the beast.

Alright, so the FGBF (Former Gay Best Friend), we will call him Harry. He was foreign, British, and was a former model. He had even competed on a Gay reality television program.

All of that should have been a red flag for me.

All of it.

Why?

Anyone who goes on reality television, complaining for years afterward they were loved by everyone, and the whole thing was staged, well, they are spiritually bypassing. Unable or unwilling to accept how the situation played out as being what it was meant to be, so the choice is to cling to it and decide it is a wrong from the world becomes spiritual bypassing. He could have chosen to see his perspective was coloring his belief of the world's resistance to him, when in reality he was resisting the world. He could have, and perhaps he still will at some point. It was not for me to force into his awareness. It was something he needed to see for himself.

This opinion I formed was after many hours and days of going over all the things I wish I had said. I wanted to bring these things to his awareness, yet I knew every time I made an attempt to show him a part of his persona or behavior that wasn't in alignment with his words, I would be attacked. Conversations were cut off, and it became something that exhausted me continually.

His name on my phone's Caller ID started giving me anxiety attacks. After I turned off my notifications, I started noticing moments I would feel utterly physically drained. I always had messages from him waiting for me.

My spiritual alarm system was showing me a drain on my energy, showing me something not meant to continue. I still dragged it out. I wanted to believe the best of him, but I couldn't take the continual negativity. Brutal honesty, I could not take one more conversation hearing about the rigged voting from the show he didn't win.

That was me back when I wanted to focus on the custody case I was involved in during the majority of 2020. I could sit and continually complain about the judge, bitch that my lawyer was shit, the arguments were garbage, it was all staged and a ploy for money, and so on.

Or I could choose to see it made my relationship with my children bulletproof. It made me stand up for myself, and fight for my dreams and my life. It made George ridiculously aware he could no longer abuse me nor the kids and get away with it. I didn't lose custody of my children, and that means I won the case. Why should I continue to bitch?

We all hold onto certain "wrongs" we perceive happened to us. It is an opportunity in a moment like this one, right here, to challenge your own perception. Can you see what you are holding onto? Is it something from high school? Is it something from childhood? Is it something that happened at the supermarket last week that for whatever reason served to reaffirm a distorted perception of people being out to get you?

Whatever it is you are holding onto, you have a chance now, tomorrow, and even had the chance yesterday to shift the perception into clarity. Something I have learned when I asked Spirit for clarity it is always given. It is up to me to accept the clarity given. It is up to me to challenge the ways in which my mind will twist the truth being shown into what serves my lower ego self.

Perception shifts into reality are in your hands. You have the ultimate power to see things in a different way, to change and adapt your truth and bring clarity and peace to your mind and heart. You hold that power for yourself. It doesn't require me sitting here telling you, though I am a firm believer in Spirit leading us all to the lessons we need to learn, even if they come from another.

This means if you are sitting here wondering if it is possible you have that kind of power within you, and my words are creating a stirring within your heart and soul, it means you already know you do. This is the beauty of Spirit speaking to you through the words of another. I love how this works, because I communicate with Spirit and the Universe in exactly this way myself.

Before we jump back into the chaos and purging, bitch-fest, I want to say thank you. I am honored to be able to be one of your synchronicities. I am honored to be one who brings you back to the understanding of your own inner power, simply through the stories I tell. Those of you who feel this way, you're a motivation for me, even when I don't know you personally. You bring to me another layer to my sense of purpose in the world. Thank you.

Okay, how about we get back to the glib cynical lessons?

3

Now I have the deal with the FGBF, this whole "reality television failure to win" was something that hit so hard it was a continual conversation we had. UGH! Okay, I am not going to continue to bitch about it.

Here's what happened. It was a good relationship until it wasn't. He was egotistical and wouldn't allow himself to see it. Quite literally he endured putting an elderly dog down, and it was as though the biggest trauma of his life happened.

I am in no way, shape, or form diminishing the loss of a pet. As I mentioned in "Brutal Warning," I have a new puppy, but only because we had to put down my dog. My baby. I had her through my divorce. Saved her from a horrible situation. All of it.

It was a beautiful journey with her and suddenly we were told we would have 6 months to a year with her and it was less than a week later we were putting her down. It was the right thing but horribly painful.

So when I say, I understand the pain, *I understand the pain*. It has been a year now since we have put Molly-dog down. I know how enduringly hard the pain is. Yet when it was about the loss of his dog, as though his whole life was ending, he unilaterally decided it was 100% my job to be there for him every second of every day.

I wasn't allowed to spend the time I informed him I was spending for myself. I was attacked for spending time with my best friend and nephew after not seeing them for a year and a half. I was attacked for going on an inner self-healing journey after being led by my guides.

I can't even tell you when it was, we hit the point of the relationship in which I found myself back in the throes of the narcissistic/empath dynamic I had endured for so long. He always told me he was an empath. He cried on the phone with me. Wanted me to praise him, be indignant for him, and heal him. At the very least, these are the impressions given from his actions. His words spoke a dramatically different story.

---

*Of note: It isn't lost on me that as I continue to move through this situation, more realizations are coming in I wasn't able to see earlier. My guides sent me message after message, up to yesterday about Covert Narcissists, and I failed to draw the correlations. As I sat editing and working through the memories all of this has brought to the surface, I cannot help but finally draw a correlation for closure I wasn't able to prior.

Sometimes we doubt ourselves and our own awareness and intuition. I was terrible with this. I have always believed I am an excellent judge of character, and I can read people easily. I can. I can read energy, and I have heard from multiple people how accurate (bordering on scary) what I read from others energy is.

Thinking back to Hope, my best friend, who told me emphatically in January of 2020, I needed to learn to read auras. I always see the best in people, and I needed to learn to read auras. Her message resounding once more in my head as I look over this.

Then I saw the image of the years I had to verify through multiple people, messages I would receive from George and Wendy, insecurity about my own perceptive awareness leading me to need others to confirm I was experiencing what I already knew to be the truth.

It wasn't until my journey into editing this book, I saw the memory replay in my head. The times I needed to screenshot messages and send them to David. The messages I showed my best friend as she was visiting me over Christmas 2021. The need internally for outer confirmation that I was not in the wrong. People pleasing again.

I am finding, sometimes the most subtle of habits are the ones hardest to break. Even more so, they are the hardest to truly see as indicators of how we attach our identities and self-worth to the opinions of other people.

It is in those memories, I find myself abundantly grateful for the people who will confirm my own inner knowing, and then tell me how silly and foolish I am for not trusting myself. It is pure love, pure support, and true friendship shining forth in every one of those memories.

It got to the point that he tried to make me feel guilty about the fact that he supposedly was bit by a poisonous spider, landed in the hospital, and almost died. Something that would have been an emergent kind of notification thing. He messaged me at 3 am, my time, when he had to rush his dog to the vet.

Yet when he almost died from a poisonous spider bite, he didn't message me until three days later?

To me, it was the last straw. This man was supposed to be my friend. I was in the wrong for spending time with other people. I was in the wrong for prioritizing my own healing. I was in the wrong for focusing on my family and my children. I was in the wrong to him.

To me, it is nauseating how he approached me with his self-centered, narrow view. To me it felt like he was nothing but a spoiled person who believed everyone owed him something. I didn't owe him a thing. He also believed he is Archangel Michael incarnated.

Unfortunately, I have to own the fact that I did that too. I pushed that because of a story he made up about his dead aunt who messaged him on Facebook, a picture of an angel, despite not having an account before she died, and it just miraculously appearing in his inbox.

Is it possible?

Sure, but after all the lies and manipulation from him, I seriously don't believe a word he has ever said in his and my interactions. As you can see through the words I am writing here, this man was someone I loved someone who hurt me deeply. Someone I no longer am able to have in my life.

There is an issue we all have to come to discover within our lives, as well as within society. It is all about words and actions. You see, I told you all of the childish drama between Harry and I, but did you catch what the biggest lesson was through all the bullshit?

The biggest issue is that I was listening to the words he was saying and not accounting for his actions. I was paying attention only to the specific words versus the words left unsaid, the ones floating in the liminal quietness between breaths. It is in the subtle we find the truth, not amongst the noise. It is in the actions taken, whether or not they become confirmatory of the words and theories and beliefs espoused, or whether they are contradictory.

Ask yourself when you feel the sliver of doubt in what you are feeling and experience, is this contradictory or confirmatory? Does this person's actions, or do my own actions contradict what I have been saying? Do they confirm what I have been saying?

If I come to you and tell you I am a psychic, but I do not nurture and use my gifts every day, am I not being contradictory? Would you believe me if I told you I was a psychic, but I only announced it without evidence to the contrary?

This is one of the greatest challenges. Believing something taboo and not being willing to back up that belief when challenged. Christianity has had martyrs all throughout history. Would you be able to believe someone unwilling to fall on their own sword for what they believe in fully?

I have fallen on my sword too many times to count. I am always going to be willing to do that. I will tell you how I feel and what I believe, and I will walk my talk. If I don't, call me out. If we find a common ground through a reasonable discussion, this is how we move forward on equal footing. If we continue to fight, we will part ways. It is quite simple honestly.

It is something I am continually learning in life. Actions versus words. Confirmatory versus contradictory. It is something we are all working to learn, both in ourselves and in others.

-4-

When I am hurt, I hurt others back. Something to note, and definitely something I needed to open my eyes to, is I can be mean as well. While I know I can control myself around other people, in the silence and aloneness, I am still capable of being mean to other people. It isn't something I am proud of, but yes, it definitely is something of which I am capable.

I could continue going on this Harry-centered bitch fest. Honestly though, this is a cautionary tale. It isn't about stranger danger either. It is about you. This is a cautionary tale to teach you about you, and no one else.

How many times in your life have you sat there and wondered why someone lied to you?

How many times in your life have you sat and wondered why someone used you?

How many times have you wondered why someone was selfish and hurtful?

Wondering "why," was a pattern I too easily fell into. I am continually trying to understand human motivation. The hidden reasons behind the hurtful behaviors others (and I) engage in. It was absolutely a major proponent of my first book. I don't do that now.

More often than not, in my opinion, most of the adult behaviors I find myself questioning are easily tied to some childhood wounding pattern. For Harry, I knew it had to do with him feeling utterly unwanted and unloved. I truly wish he could have realized the way these shadows came forth in his actions now, but I was not meant to be the one to help him to see it.

Stop wondering about them. I could have sat and torn myself apart about Harry. I didn't. I chose not to. Don't tear yourself down in order to understand why someone else wasn't who they originally presented themselves as.

It creates a negative biofeedback loop in your mind, strengthening the misfiring of your brain from your prior pains. Get yourself out of that by seeing you have control over your actions and reactions, but not those of others.

Do you have a Harry in your own life? I wouldn't be surprised if you could locate one for yourself. I have a friend who would tell me that my Harry is her Katrina and Corbin.

Absolutely it would be the truth. People who believe those who have suffered from trauma or those who are genuine giving and kind people, they make easy targets.

Katrina and Corbin contain a cautionary tale in and of themselves. The only reason I know of the fraudulent activity is because of my friend (whose name I am choosing to omit for her own protection). She came to me after dealing with these two for several months, and her life was on the cusp of falling apart entirely.

The programs promoted through the actions of these two, let alone the clear false claims of expertise on their public websites were blatantly obvious to me, however, they have tactics to approaching people. It is methodical, calculated, and truly terrifying.

I am telling you this because these are people who are examples of a group of humanity, we need to open our eyes to. This is the group who know how to prey on traumas. They know how to create illusions with influential words and carefully constructed lies.

They are the people who seemingly get away with taking thousands of dollars from other people, victimizing them, traumatizing them, and work through fear in healing's clothing, just like a wolf in sheep's clothing. I honestly have never seen anything like it.

How they are able to do this, they find people, subtly coerce them, create illusions of friendship, and then they attempt to push certain behaviors, much like dictators do. Their entire design is to create confusion and doubt to make money, and they do all this through using false identities and lies.

If you take nothing else from all this, take the truth of yourself to the bank from here on out: YOU ARE NOT AN EASY TARGET.

If you are an empath, use it as your superpower. You can tell when someone is lying. Stop doubting yourself because they seem smooth and just tell them to fuck right off. That is what I should have done with Harry. It is what my friend should have done with Katrina and Corbin. It is what you should do with Maria, Whitney, or Carl, whoever it is that you have on your list of Harry's.

Fuck the people who want to hurt you and take advantage of you. Do you think that I really should have continued to be involved in such an overly dramatic friendship?

Absolutely fucking not.

I made a point in my life to walk the fuck away from drama a long time prior to it, but it was like all the life lessons I *knew* I had learned suddenly disappeared from my mind in 2021.

Fucking hell.

There is a saying, I will have to look it up quickly, so I quote it proper.

Give me a moment . . .

Just about there . . .

Ah! I found it!

"Do not take life too seriously. You will never get out of it alive."

– Elbert Green Hubbard, writer and philosopher

I wish I could insert my favorite meme right here. Good ol' Morgan Freeman, pointing up and saying, "He's right you know?" or she depending on the situation. Regardless, this is the perfect moment for that.

And yes, I use memes and emojis for emphasis. My husband and I have complete conversations in gif form as well. It is what it is. Sometimes you have to engage in the simple things in life, you know? So, yeah, when you are on the drama train all the time, everything in life is nothing but serious.

It is dramatic. It is over the top, complete, and utter fuckery. It sucks! It sucks up one way and down the other. Which is arguably one of my favorite sayings to use when I really want to emphasize how much something sucks. Do I know how it would work logistically? Nope. No clue.

Just because life is all of those things, doesn't mean we should take all the seriousness into ourselves. We all need to learn to laugh more, live more, and let go of the people that bring all that dramatic fuckery into our lives. Myself included.

-5-

Back to you and what you are learning here. Number one, why aren't you talking about the shit you have been through? Here I am risking it all, letting people see me as a whiny bitch without being able to give a flying fuck what it is anyone thinks because I am speaking my fucking truth here.

We spend way too much of our lives not speaking out about the bullshit. Partly, at least for me, I was worried about karma. I was worried if I were to lay all this out for the world to see that I would get smacked down by karma. The other part, well it has everything to do with conditioned fear.

Where has keeping silent about people wronging others gotten anyone? Seriously. I want you to ask yourself that right now.

I can wait . . .

Let me know, I'm curious about what it is that you have found as an answer. For me, staying silent about all of this has made me not want to be a lightworker. It has made me want to withhold my light from the world. It has made me not want to use my gifts and not want to walk my path.

Why?

Because people can be assholes. So can I.

How does it make me any different?

It makes me different, and if you are reading this and it resonates (a fancy word for it fits way too fucking well with your own story) then it makes you different too. You, like me, really just want people to see we have the ability to **not** be assholes to each other all the time. It doesn't mean we have to be self-centered, but we have to take care of ourselves first and foremost.

Each one of us on this fucking journey somehow fall into the trap of being of service. When you haven't gotten to the point in which you realize you are being of service by taking care of yourself, you can too easily end up sacrificing yourself.

Don't sacrifice your truth, your voice, or your life for someone else. It isn't worth it. Even if you are doing it in the name of love. That is not what love really is about.

Unconditional love is the epitome of real love. It is the love we all talk about, but too few of us understand.

When you become the lion, you understand that unconditional love means you allow the person to do what they need to for themselves, and you still love them through it.

You don't require them to be something more than they are.

You don't require them to sacrifice their dreams for your own.

You don't require yourself to sacrifice you and your dreams for ANYONE.

For any of you who are parents, and you are scoffing at me right now because "If I were a parent, I would know that kids come first." No, honey, no they don't. When you live that life, you teach them to do the same thing you are doing. You teach them their life doesn't matter in comparison to other people.

I have four children. I know. I taught my kids, and then had to unteach them that lesson. I had to teach them to go against all I had conditioned them to believe because I had been conditioned to believe other people always mattered above and beyond myself.

Harry was great for teaching me this lesson. He taught me it wasn't worth it for me to be involved in a friendship resulting in a drain on my energy and resources because it made someone else happy. He was just one of many who treated me that way. I will never engage in friendships like that again.

I do not allow myself to wait for someone to see my worth. They aren't meant to be in my life if they are incapable of giving back to me equally how I give to them. If you haven't learned by now, then learn from me here.

Vet the people in your life.

Do what you need to do.

Protect your energy.

And I don't mean doing ritual after ritual.

Don't overcomplicate it. I did that once.

I mean, know your worth and don't falter from it. When someone approaches you to speak to you about the shit is going on in their life, and then continues to use you over and over again without giving you an equal safe space, cut them out. When someone uses you and then takes from you trying to silence you, cut them the fuck out. It doesn't matter how much you love them. You need to love yourself more.

No one in the world came into the world with the same energy, gifts, and beauty as you. No one is going to leave the world when you do. Seriously. That whole you were born alone and die alone thing, it is kind of applicable here.

No one has to live in your brain.

No one has to live with your choices the way you do.

If you are the one that has to live with the pieces within yourself, don't be the lamb, be the mother fucking lion.

Be the warrior.

Be the fucking light.

Fight Fire with Fire

-1-

Fire, let it fucking burn! Have you ever found yourself wanting to burn everything in your life down? I have. I have been there far too many times. I have found myself building something and becoming so frustrated with the progress, I simply wanted to say, "Fuck it all."

Burn it all to the ground and walk away from the ashes knowing there wouldn't be a phoenix rising because it wasn't meant to be. What fucking pain there is in that moment.

These times come when you have been knocked down and out time and again, and you keep fucking going. You don't know how you are going anymore, but it is like you have somehow found yourself in the state of, "I don't know what else to do. I don't know how to not keep moving forward."

I told David exactly that sentiment not too long ago. I had hit a low lower than I have felt in years. I looked at him, bawling my eyes out, and said, "I don't know how to not keep pushing forward. I don't know how to not keep going."

To his credit he most definitely worked to make me feel better about it, "That's a good thing though, isn't it?"

And he wasn't wrong. (Don't tell him I said that though!)

It most definitely was a good thing. If I didn't know how to keep going, I wouldn't be here, writing all this shit out. I wouldn't be working on getting it out of me, hoping and trying once more to shed light on the truth of life, love, spirituality, trauma, and overcoming. All these things I am trying to help others with, all things I have had to help myself with.

Want to know the brutal truth? Fuck, I have been all about laying out the brutal truths in this book, why stop now?

I can tell you my stories and share my lessons. I can uplift you. I can tell you all the things you already know are true within yourself. None of that will change how you see and feel about yourself. It will all be things you have heard and will need to tell yourself continually.

You are the one who will heal you. And that isn't meant to make you feel as though you are all alone in this, fuck that shit.

If you were, I wouldn't be writing this. No, you aren't alone, but I do not want the credit for your healing. I want you to own the fuck out of your own healing because you are the one who came to read this. You are the one who needed this. You are the one.

It's like you are Neo and I am Morpheus. I am here to give you the choice of the Red or the Blue pills, but you are the one who has to choose which one to take. That also means you are the one who needs to take your own power into your own hands.

Neo changed the Matrix. Not Morpheus, but Neo. So you are the proverbial ONE. It is for you to make the changes and to burn down the structure of the old you. To fight fire with fire. If someone wants to burn you, if the world wants to burn you, burn it back. Blaze your fucking light so brightly it is going to scorch the eyes of the clouded, and let your life be what it is meant to be.

Alright enough of the metaphor bullshit, let's do some more real talk. The most prominent moment in my recent past of wanting to burn the living fuck out of everything in my life came in 2020. Let me tell you right here and now, when you feel that way, even just the one time, it fucking lingers. It lingers like the stale smell of cigarette smoke after a night out bar hopping.

Granted these days, it isn't the best analogy, but you want to know what? I remember when you could smoke indoors. I remember smelling like cigarette smoke when I would come home from nights out with my ladies. I remember the way George would bitch incessantly at me as if I were a piece of shit to him, and he just couldn't seem to find the flushing mechanism in life for.

Good ol' George. He's the first one who led me to beg and plead with the higher forces to break me the fuck out. Get me the fuck out.

Please for the love of God, do not make me incur the karmic retribution of having to disappear into thin air, kind of mentality.

I can be a very loving person, intensely forgiving, and I will give a person more chances than well, shit I don't have an accurate analogy of the number of chances because I don't think it exists. I used to believe it was because I was weak-willed. In the past, it would have been a pseudo true statement. Only pseudo true because I know it was because I believe in others. I believe I can show others a better way to be, and because I always try to see the best in others.

What are you supposed to think or feel when you have given people the chance to not be a complete douche and all they seem to do is be a bigger one than before you gave them the chance to change?

Burn it all fucking down!

2

George and I were in the middle of a wicked custody battle. He told the courts because he worked full time, outside the house, and I am a stay-at-home mother, who is always there for my children, he is a better, more suitable parent. Granted, he added the accusation I was homebound, never showed up for my children, and came just shy of calling me neglectful.

He also "diagnosed" me with bipolar disorder manifesting in mood swings in which I refuse to allow him to see the children. Ridiculously specific manner in which that mental health disorder presents itself, don't you think?

Not that I am downplaying bipolar disorder, but well, George never graduated college, never studied Psychology (which would be my area of expertise, so to speak), and most definitely never went to medical school. Zero right for that accusation is the understatement of the century.

By all accounts, there should have been zero cause for me to feel fear from this man. Except it was ingrained in me to fear him. Until this situation. It was through this I found the anger I had been shoving down, the indignation, and the laughability of the ways he twisted everything in order to avoid taking any sort of responsibility.

As I have said before, we are meant to feel every one of our emotions. They are all a part of the human experience. When we feel small, diminished by another, it is in these moments the anguish we experience is teaching us.

We are learning, if we choose to open our eyes wider, to actually see the reality. We are learning to see when a person speaking against us, and to use it as the chance to rise above. I wasn't fully healed in 2020. I started my journey "late in the game" in my opinion. Perhaps it wasn't though. If it were not for the way it played out, I may never have found the inner fire I needed to bring me right here, to this very moment, sharing all of this with the world.

As we sat in the court room, the day prior to Christmas eve, George's lawyer made his grand sweeping closing argument to the courts, "There are child molesters and murderers who get more facetime with their children than my client does."

At the end of the day, it was the judge's words that led me to, *it's time to burn this fuck of a place to the mother fucking ground*.

"You're right, there are child molesters and murderers who see their children more. Visitation is to resume with alternating weekends for the next six months. Both parties are ordered to have Psychological Evaluations, and George is ordered to have an Anger Management evaluation. George, you are to establish family therapy sessions for you and the children jointly. I am also ordering David to spend Christmas Day with George, Wendy, and the children."

SCREECH!

WHAT IN THE LITERAL FUCK JUST HAPPENED?!

Out in the hallway, my daughter, who had been called in to testify only to have the judge put her on the stand, swear her in, and tell her he wasn't going to allow her to speak, while simultaneously praising me as a mother for teaching her to share her story and use her voice, was waiting.

Upon me and her lawyer sitting and telling her the news, she began screaming bloody murder, "NO! NO! NO! NO!" Right as the judge exited the room. Everyone in the courthouse heard her fear and her anguish that afternoon, including the judge who had decided to send her back to her abuser.

Now, I could sit here and bitch to high heaven about the simple fact that a family judge decided to induce parental alienation with his decision. I could. However, it was only a moment in time. It was, among many others, a lesson about what manifestation is and is not possible. I couldn't have impacted on a spiritual or energetic level what happened in that court room. The Grand Conjunction between Jupiter and Saturn was occurring. I had just begun my journey of discovery with astrology, and all I knew about what the heavens were ushering in, was my life was about to change.

Did I realize both George and the judge, not to mention Wendy, their lawyer, my lawyer, and yes, even myself all were energetically impacted by a healthy level of expansive karmic rebalancing during that time?

Fuck no.

All I knew was I was left out of Christmas with my family. I was spending it alone, and my children had to return to the house of horrors they had been living in for far too long. Instead of wallowing in the pain on Christmas Day, I started writing in a gratitude journal. Every part of me was changing and growing, breaking free from what and who I was *before*.

I will thank Spirit and the Universe until the day I die, my children were not removed from my custody, but I still look back at that time and wonder what the fuck the point of it is. Perhaps it's something I will learn later on down the road in life? Perhaps it was too vast of a rebalance for me to see all the interplay.

Whatever it was, I walked out of that room, and there was a feeling in the middle of my chest, blossoming like the newly opened rose bud in the early days of summer. Only this feeling was far less majestic, and significantly closer to sheer panic.

I couldn't send them back!

I couldn't return to being powerless and abused!

I could not do this all over again! How could I be asked to do this? Why would my children be forced back to that home?

Round and round the mental hamster would run on the wheel in my brain. I would replay every moment in that room for months. Breaking it all down, trying to find myself some sort of loophole, some sign of misconduct. It only made the panic worse. I wanted to burn my life to the mother fucking ground.

I wanted to destroy everything I had been doing, change my phone number, change my name, delete all my social media, and disappear. Seriously, this is how much I want to save my children from dealing with the man who created so much trauma in my life it took me more than a decade to take all my power back from him.

3

The years prior to court had been the hardest of my life as a mother. Watching my daughter go from being happy, bubbly, and outgoing, never questioning her worth or her body, to battling eating disorders and mental health illnesses.

Hearing my seven-year-old son confess to our entire family he had been scratching himself because he was scared of taking showers after his stepmother continually invaded his privacy and forced him to allow her to bathe him. Listening to a child psychiatrist tell me, my 12-year-old daughter had five, **FIVE** different mental illness diagnoses, all tied to trauma and abuse. It was the most helpless feeling I had ever experienced.

My mind continued to swirl round and round. The worries compounding the stress and anxiety, and vice versa. I had watched both my children endure things they never should have had to, powerless to help them, despite every effort. It was as though I was a rapid dog, cornered, frightened, and the judicial system just handed George the gun of my undoing. Something had to give. Anything.

Do you know the saying: *Don't get mad, get even?*

That is what I did, in my own way. I didn't run from all this shit. I wasn't a coward. Instead I hit it head on. I was strong. I was resilient. I stood my ground and I stood in my power. I even tried discussing with George, offering to sit down and talk it all out for the sake of the children.

He told me it was all my fault, and essentially intimated I had a lot to "make up" for before he would consider doing anything that would better the children, and bridge the gap of parenting between him and I.

It is a sad thing, truly, for me to see the father of my children who cannot allow for growth to happen despite every attempt made. It is sad to me to know my story and my children's story is not a unique one.

It is something happening far too often in our world. Children more adult than the parents who have brought them into this world, and by societal standards, stuck with being the mature leaders, sacrificing their childhoods because the justice system values genetics over truth.

George is one of those parents. He never can take ownership and responsibility for his actions. Even just sitting here writing this for you all, I can feel that same sense of panic. That, *what is he going to bring to my doorstep next*, burgeoning fear in my chest.

I am sitting here, making myself take deep, even breaths. I know it is residual. I know he doesn't have control over me. I know I can protect my children no matter what.

Welcome to trauma from an abuser. He will never own it, but it is who and what he is anyway. So how do you continually deal with it? How do you overcome it?

First off, don't fucking burn your life to the ground.

The only thing accomplished is assuring the other person wins the power you have been working so diligently to take into your own hands. Even when Harry set out to destroy the business I have built, to bury my YouTube channel, relegating it to the fringes of the algorithm, and then to personally attack me as though I forced him to become suicidal again. Well, even then I didn't burn my life down.

Instead of burning my life to the ground, I took inventory. What mattered to me and what didn't. What felt right and what drained me. What tethered my energy to an old version of myself and what did the person I truly am desire. I walked away from what was no longer helping but hindering me and my life. I walked my happy ass away from all that didn't serve anymore, and I did it for both situations.

Don't get mad, get even.

If someone talks shit about you, and/or they seek to take your power from you, they do all the fucked-up bullshit you know will eventually come back at them in some form, fucking let it happen. Don't show them they have any power over you. Keep fucking doing what is right for you, every single step forward. Shine your beautiful fucking light without question or hesitation.

Don't get mad, get even.

I wrote a book. I told the world about what I went through. I shared with the world the anguish of my daughter because her grandfather Barty and George were birds of a feather, equally attacking her for speaking her truth to them about how she was traumatized by both of them. The court applauded her for wanting to speak her truth and then silenced her. I gave her back her voice.

This is what it means to get even.

It **doesn't** mean to shoot back when you are being shot at.

It **doesn't** mean to hit back when someone hits you.

Getting even is speaking the truth into existence.

You tell everyone and anyone in whatever way you feel is right. This isn't about gossip and yapping your mouth on the streets. What is this whole fucking chapter? It is me speaking the truth.

Let's go on a slight tangent here – because I guarantee there are those who are going to use the gossip angle to attempt to discount what I am saying here. Again, my guides were WAY ahead of you all. I came across a meme about gossip just the other day, and because I am a stickler for definitions and semantics, I immediately took to being absolutely crystal clear on the word.

Gossip is telling stories based in falsehood about other people. There is not a single part of gossip that involves the truth. In fact, the word itself has no origins tying it to how we define it now. It's origins are all about pouring out, as in the pouring out of spirit. Oh how we have misconstrued things.

I had this very conversation with my mom after I learned the origins of the word. We were talking about this book, and I told her about the signs and the lesson I was guided to learn. (Again, I am going to emphasize here the level of comfort I feel talking with my Christian, Lutheran mother about Spirit Guides, channeling, psychic visions, and spirituality. For anyone out there who thinks there is some sort of separation between which version of God you choose to believe in over others, this is a lesson important to learn. It matters not what God you choose to believe in, as all versions are the same. What matters is love. Only love. Always love. Don't misconstrue shit.)

When I told her the meaning of the word was to "pour our Spirit," as in channeling and speaking Divine Truth into the physical world, her response highlights perfectly the problem humanity faces too often. She said, "That's not what it means anymore!"

Fucking Telephone Game hits again! We have a choice when we have a perception creating dissonance and discomfort within us based on the actions or thoughts of others. We can either stay in the perception we have been living in, make judgements upon others, and lord our "Super Duper Selves" over them. Or we could make an attempt to learn outside the box we have been living in. Me, I am always one learning. The perpetual student. Give me a new perspective, allow me the time to mull it over so I am able to bring the balance to the inner shake-up occurring from the change, and see how we are able to find deeper communication together.

Telephones are a beautiful invention meant to connect people. When it becomes a game of who said what, without anyone breaking out of their own perception, well, there is clearly nothing but static on the line. Don't allow for communication to be a game. Let it flow freely how it is meant. If you have attempted everything you know to do, and there is the perpetual discord, walk the fuck away.

None of this is meant, in any way, to shit talk Harry, Barty, nor George. This is a pouring out of my spirit as I work collaboratively with Spirit. There is actually an incredibly important lesson layered in all this chaotic bullshit.

When shit hits the fan, and you want to tear down and destroy all the things that really matter in your life because you feel the world is against you, and you cannot *breathe* around the fear and panic, you find what your golden ticket to relief is.

Tell your story.

Tell your truth.

Share it out and don't worry about what anyone else says, thinks, or does. Why should their opinions matter more than your voice? Why do opinions hold more weight than truth?

4

Fighting fire with fire, yeah, this is what it looks like. You forgive the person who burned you. You forgive them over and over and over and over again. Do you get my drift here? I know I am being redundant. You don't just forgive them. You HAVE to forgive yourself. You shouldn't give another person an allowance you will not give to yourself. They get your power, and you stay a victim.

YOU ARE NOT A FUCKING VICTIM.

Don't let another person make you feel like you are. Pull your grown-up panties up past your fucking belly button like the rest of us cool moms and dads (mostly moms, we are just way cooler), and own your life. Own your truth.

Set fire to the shit from the past that doesn't reflect who you truly are. You want to be the truest rockstar that you are within.

Don't hesitate.

Don't hold back.

Don't allow a single other person to tell you that you aren't meant to do, be, or feel anything.

You don't give anyone an inch when it comes to how they treat you. If you know what your worth is, you know how you are meant to be treated. You have the right to tell whoever is in your life that isn't respecting you to kick rocks.

Yes, you really can do that. Yes, you can. Quit fucking arguing with me. You know the truth; you have the power to tell someone no. So, tell them FUCK NO, and walk the fuck away.

Or do like I did, write a fucking book about all the bullshit. Hell write two books. Write three of them. Not a writer? Start a podcast. Try videos. If none of those are appealing, then go stand on a street corner and scream to the masses about whatever douchebag you are dealing with. Go fucking big here.

Just do what you need to for you without worrying about what that other asshole is going to say.

Fight fire with fire.

Burn brighter.

Fucking blaze into the world.

Noise Cancelling Bullshit

1

Have you ever noticed the outside world has a distinctive noise level to it? For real, like a background humming of bullshit always running, never fading, and torturing every level of your peace of mind. If you didn't notice it before, I bet you will now. It wasn't something I was aware of in the beginning of my spiritual journey either.

I spent most of my life with the television or the radio on. Needing some form of background noise. I never realized it was because when there wasn't that kind of noise in the background, there were voices perpetually whispering in my ears.

Fuck! Am I crazy?! HA! I wish, for real, I would love a vacation at one of those "mental health spas" all the movie stars go to. I think most "normal" people really could use one of those vacations. I can see it now, people lined up out the door, each one of us a card-carrying "crazy" person.

One of us can hear disembodied voices, another feels the pains of other people, and better yet, those who can see and speak to spirits. Well fuck, all those who are psychic are just overstressed and crazy.

Here is the thing, we are all psychic. You are psychic. Your mom is psychic. Even the asshole who was tailgating the fuck out of your car last Tuesday in the carpool lane while his car was fucking empty, and he was just trying to skip the backed-up traffic while you were in your minivan with Susie's five other friends screaming and giggling, is psychic.

Damn, that was a wicked visual I was just served up. Funny thing about that is I know what I saw, what I described, it will match one of you to a T. You'll think, *Fuck, that asshole must be psychic because that is EXACTLY what happened last Tuesday* while simultaneously getting pissed because you want "superpowers," and not fully realizing that you are psychic.

Yes, I started it off by telling you that, but you got caught up in the background noise. So how the fuck do you cancel this shit out? Noise canceling headphones will do nothing but make you listen to your own shallow breathing which will just create another insecurity about you not breathing deeply enough. Fucking hell, can we get a break from all the insecurities and bullshit of regulatory notions of how we are meant to live our lives yet?

Nope.

Fucking background noise.

Are you beginning to understand the nature of what the background noise of the world really is like?

It isn't strictly about the television, nor music, nor is it anything one would normally attribute to it. Background noise in the world is less about the noise, and more about what we are told to focus on, what we are told is important, and what we are made to believe of ourselves and our place in this world.

Half the time we hear we shouldn't read fiction, shouldn't watch television, shouldn't watch movies because it is a distraction from real life and part of the "Matrix."

After that, it is avoid social media but you have to maintain a certain level of presence when you are building a business, teaching others, and even as an author. So what are we to do with all the duplicitous information? All the fucking background noise?

Cancel it all the fuck out.

Don't allow for the background noise of a single other person to dictate what it is you engage in. If you are losing yourself in wine but never watch a single moment of television, are you not engaging in the same thing? Who gives a flying fuck (sidenote: what is a flying fuck and who would give one or why would it be given? If you have the answer to this, please, let me know, but only if you do it via skywriting planes)?

Did you just get distracted thinking about what a flying fuck actually is? Wondering about the cost of a skywriting plane, and do they even still have skywriting planes? Background noise, my dear, background noise. It is so easy for us to allow ourselves to be blinded to the truth when all the background noise of the world is pressuring us from every side.

Don't allow me to sit here and dictate what it is you engage in to relax and unwind. Fuck, if I had listened to every spiritual teacher, I ran my way across (and believe you me there were a lot of them), then I would be sitting alone in the woods, wearing all natural fabrics, eating twigs and leaves, and a complete and utter recluse. I wouldn't be communicating with my guides, and I would have ended my marriage and run from my family.

FUCK THAT!

Shit, this is why all spiritual teachers in the world need a healthy dose of realistic responsibility. Can you tell me in all honesty what you are touting is absolutely what you believe? Would you end a happy marriage because of some fucked up spiritual notion twin flames require "separation," all the while you are touting the belief of the Universal Law of Oneness?

How do they not see the spiritual bypassing?

How do they not understand the lessons they are teaching hold the potential to destroy happiness and real love, creating yet another illusion?

To tell you the truth, I don't think a single one of them really cares. It is why I stepped my happy ass away from the direct spiritual teaching role and began developing new methods and techniques designed to share my stories but allow for personal interpretation and the freedom to decide for oneself.

I don't promote my shit as being the end-all-be-all truth of the world. Fuck no. It is my truth and mine alone. Some of it may resonate with you. Some of it may be the most relieving moment for you to read. At last, someone is finally telling the fucking truth about all this bullshit and the people who pretend their way through the ones genuinely out here doing good things.

---

*Of note:** As I was re-editing – it's not a one and done kind of process – I find myself contemplating another truth of mine. Truth, personal truths, they are changeable. Everything in the world is structured and built around two constants: Change and Love. I have changed my truth many times. I have learned what was necessary for a situation or time in my life, and it served my growth. When the growth has come to an end, and I begin settling into this truth, this is the moment my guides always come in to help me see *more*.

More is always going to be there, so perhaps it should be included in the list of constants. How ironic, right? I just stated a truth of two constants yet discovered a third. This is the exact nature of truth. Truth is always going to be subject to change. It changes as we do.

When we hold to a truth that is nothing more or less than a lie, even if it did not start out that way, we choose. Are we going to keep holding onto it, or are we going to allow for change to occur and more to come in? I choose change. I choose more. Every time.

Sometimes the background noise needs to be cancelled.

How do you cancel out all the fucking background noise?

2

Figure out how the universe speaks to you. Focus your efforts on communication first. This will open the dialogue, between you and Spirit, you and your Spirit Guides, you and whatever deity you commune with.

I went to dinner with my daughters one night. We went to a local wings restaurant. While there wasn't really any drama, no overly rambunctious group or crowd, there was a surplus of energetic background noise occurring the entire time. It was like a steady humming of energy running its way through my nervous system, winding and wrapping around, and through my entire body.

It started with a low murmur.

As the murmur grew, my appetite waned, my patience faltered, and every semblance of calm and serenity began to ebb away from my firm inner centeredness. This is the nature of the background noise in the world.

We think it is something we can hear clearly, like the wailing of a child as the parents are ignoring them for the sake of whatever is going on in the cyber world, and the rest of the world has to suffer through the ear-piercing screams. That is not how it really is. There is a background noise to the background noise.

It is the opinions, the beliefs, the mentality of others whose perspectives are so fucking skewed to their own narrowness nothing can come of it other than sheer toxicity upon extended time around them. It is the mentality of being better than another because of viewpoint as well. It is all the constructs we place into the world based on our perception sending out an energetic ripple creating more noise. We all partake in the background noise, and we all succumb to it in one way or another. It is a shame because the reality is we are all one, we are all connected.

Trust me when I tell you I wish nothing more or less than for that to not be my truth, but the universe served this truth up in the form of a slam me in the face torture so I would accept it. Sometimes we don't get an option. Sometimes the laws in place are there and unchangeable. This is one Universal law that can't be changed, it is sourced from the constant of Love.

What this means is, the jack ass staring into his phone instead of engaging with his toddler, yeah, he is connected to you. He impacts you. Just the same as your annoyance will spread outward through the crowd and negatively impact the waiter or waitress, the person four tables down from you who was happy and now suddenly is snapping at her boyfriend or girlfriend.

If we cannot separate our inner-self and inner-truth from the constant thrum of background noise from other people's energies, then we are all in a wicked biofeedback loop of toxicity and negativity bordering on violence much of the time.

So what the fuck do you do? Get yourself some sort of noise cancelling headphones, so to speak. Whatever it is that works for you, find it, use it. When it stops working, find something else. Don't fucking walk out the front door unless you know without a doubt you have your noise cancellers with you, and you are protected.

Why?

Because people are assholes.

We aren't supposed to be. On a soul level, we really aren't. But the unhealthy, fear-dipped, egos running around the world and running the fucking world, well they are the assholes. I am perfectly comfortable with being the one to call their selfish asses out on it.

Hey! Jack asses! Yeah, you! You know who you are! Stop with your toxic ass energy. Start being a better fucking human being. Pay attention to the needs of others and stop bitching about how the world has wronged you because of whatever twisted fucking mindset you are holding onto this week.

Do better.

Be better.

If you can't, shut the fuck up, go into what we in the tarot world like to call "Hermit mode" and find out what the fuck is going on inside of you that you are spreading this shit outward every damn day.

I want to live in a world of kitties and puppies, roses, and chocolates. I want to live in a world where we take care of each other and ourselves and no one accuses you of being selfish and we all fucking uplift each other and support one another.

That is the best fucking world I can picture, and that image is one of my pairs of noise cancelling headphones. Does it make me naïve? No, it absolutely does not.

It simply means that despite the heaping pile of cow shit I have dealt with in my life, I am still an eternal optimist who sees the best in other people, and the potential for a better life and better world. You try living optimistically when life is beating you to a fucking pulp!

Alright, so that got a lot more intense than I intended it to, but I have gotten to the point of being fed up with the world thinking that to see others in the best light means we are weak.

This is the moment I give a massive shout out to my true-blue empaths out there. I don't mean those who say, "I am an empath," because it is the "cool thing" to say these days.

No, I am talking about the ones who are like me, the ones who see the soul behind the egos.

The ones who feel the pains of the world to the extent it impacts their physical, mental, and emotional wellbeing because of all the assholes.

And if you are offended with me calling people assholes, if you are assuming I am calling you one, then stop being an asshole and you won't feel insecure and offended. Seriously, the people who get upset when called out like this are the ones who know they aren't being their "best self" and taking advantage of others.

This also seems to be the right time to talk about ego. I mention egos a lot, and I am also deeply aware of the theory of "ego death," in the world. Here is where you will find two camps of theories – those who believe the ego must die, and those who don't. For the second, my opinion is they are the ones who know better. Our egos are nothing more or less than the personality we were born into. If you believe in reincarnation (and I do), you know the ego is this incarnation. My ego is Monica. I have a soul which is eternal, but this is the only life I am going to be Monica.

An ego can be broken, it can be stuck in a state of shadow. An ego only dies when we die, or become brain dead, but that is a whole other realm we don't need to get into here. Our egos are the parts of us we build based on the conditioning we go through in life, the perspectives we form, and the person we bring into the world. It is the essence of our duality in this life, for the ego desires individuality and the soul desires unity.

An "ego death" is more like an equilibrium change. As though you have been walking through life with one of your ears having an inner ear issue and you have been off balance without knowing, for it was your natural state. When you go through awakenings, transformations, alchemization, and/or ascensions, all the fun spiritual terms for growing closer to your soul, you bring healing to your inner ear. The greater the healing, the greater equilibrium is reached.

It may lead to feeling as though we don't know ourselves and don't know what world we are living in. There can and often is confusion and fear bubbling up during these transitory healings.
All of which are normal. Sometimes, we may even undergo deeper healing moments we feel like we are going to or want to die. Then we come back to the light of day and realize we have changed and changed for the better.

We become more empathetic. We become more accepting and loving. We become more aware with a desire to make a difference. All of these things are part of what is called an "ego death." It is nothing more or less than healing. Ego healing. Ego loving. And it is beautiful.

3

We all have to learn, in order to grow and change the way our life is, we have to change how we perceive the world. We cannot change an outer perception until we change an inner perception. When we see the world as filled with manipulative assholes like I have been saying, we see ourselves as the victim of them.

I really don't feel like I should go back to telling you that you are not a victim. Flip a few chapters back and let yourself be reminded of that truth within yourself. You are not the victim of the system, nor another person. Choose to see yourself as the warrior. Yet, it is important to be careful, to be sure, your warrior is moving without reactivity.

Our emotions demand to be felt, but it is not for us to take them and lash out at other people because we are choosing to have an emotion about something or someone. Where is the emotion coming from within? What is it triggering within you? What is the root of it?

Placing blame on someone else is never the actual answer. It is about how you see the world and your place within it. The dichotomy of your own perception versus the actions and reactions of others has for too long been creating painful self-illusions holding us all back. It is time for responsibility.

When we own our own healing, when we take back the responsibility for the moments, we have lived untrue to who we truly are, and we endeavor daily to change our approach, it is then we really start to fully cancel the background noise. How ironic really.

We think there is some magic formula or secret method to living without being impacted negatively by negativity. It is just another illusion created.

We believe it is too difficult for us to take ownership because it would mean really viewing the things we have done wrong.

It takes a lot of personal strength and courage to face our inner demons rather than projecting them outward into the world. I am in a perpetual loop of shit, more or less, with George and Wendy. They want to be the victims while blaming everyone else for what they feel is a wrong having been done to them. They blame their children for standing up for themselves and reporting their abusive actions. They blame me for their children being strong and independent rather than weak-willed and subservient. I have faced the choice time after time to either continue engaging in the negative biofeedback loop or to change how I move within the bounds of coparenting.

As much as there is a part of me wanting to lash out as they do, what good would that do for me, for them, and for the children? Absolutely none. I can be glib and flippant about it, for they always present wonderful spiritual lessons on a silver platter with their words and actions, but the reality is a far cry from those reactions.

The reality is days spent on my phone as I work to help my daughter remain balanced and centered rather than wounded and reactive. Days spent fighting whether to get involved or not, knowing the response I will get is a powerful influx of blame-centered toxicity. I don't come here speaking these truths in the blatant, cynical manner I am doing for no reason. This is your shock to the system. This is your wake-up call.

I had my own, many times. I ignored them continually. Just recently I spent nearly 24 hours in a reactive then calm then reactive then calm loop. Wendy using an unborn child to emotionally and mentally harm my daughter while George stated his depression meant he was incapable of trying to see our daughter's truth for himself. All of it became this bundle of looped energy. Finally it was George lashing out at me and blaming me where it was able to break.

His blaming me was exactly what helped break me free from the biofeedback loop because it brought me back into a state of awareness. I cannot change how things impact my children. I can only teach them and guide them through it. However, if it is something coming at me, I am well aware of how to respond. I respond by becoming the mirror. I refuse to accept what blame is being attempted to be laid upon me and I return the truth right back to the person.

Here is the thing, I wasn't a perfect person. I would love to say I was, but I wasn't.

Neither was George.

None of us are perfect.

We are all perfectly who we are meant to be and doing the best we can at any given moment in time. Even George and Wendy. Even Harry. Even whoever it is in your life. It is about choosing whether the background noise of what we have too long believed we need to see and speak into the world as our truth, or choosing silence, stillness, and what is true within.

I think it is time for me, before we transition to the next stage of bitchy spiritual lessons for me to tell you the truth: everything that I am sitting here calling others out on, yeah, I have been in those shoes before.

I have been the distracted mom.

I have been the asshole who didn't give a shit about anyone outside of what I needed.

I have been the narrow minded.

I have been all those things, and I have willingly broken myself down, transformed, and gone through every level of darkness and shadow work to be a better person for myself, my family, and the whole fucking world.

I am as fucking realistic about this shit as it gets. Which is why I am perfectly comfortable with calling others out on their shit too. I do it to myself. If I am genuinely in the wrong, I will own the fuck out of it and endeavor to be a better person.

Can you say the same thing for you? If you can tell me that honestly, then we should be friends, we likely are part of what the spiritual community calls "soul family" and we definitely both get exactly what the point of this book is really about.

Let's move on.

Mid-Spiritual Life Identity Crisis

-1-

Ever wake up in the morning, you slept well, and you feel rejuvenated and ready for a new day? Then you walk in the bathroom, take one look in the mirror, and find yourself wondering, *who the fuck am I?*

Welcome to the world babe! This is a normal occurrence when you are on a spiritual journey. Spiritual identity crises come in many forms. In my experience, the worst of these are the ones that make no sense for their timing.

It is as though your world is suddenly turned back upright, everything makes perfect sense after months of chaos and hardship, and you suddenly have no clue who you are, what you are doing in your life, and for the fucking life of you, you don't know how you got to where you are right in that moment.

I have had more of these moments than not over the last decade. I remember waking up one morning, around the year 2014, and I looked over at George. I found myself wondering how the fuck I was married to this human being lying in bed with me.

I questioned how the fuck I had kids with him when looking at him in that moment made me want to vomit. What a dirty little secret of shame I carried within me during most of that marriage. I had forced myself to believe the ultimate lie, and then changed it to another lie and another until my whole life, my whole identity was nothing but a sham.

I made myself believe he was the man for me.

I made myself believe I would never love someone as I loved him.

I made myself believe he wasn't hurting me even as he raised his hands and his voice to me.

I made myself believe I was always in the wrong.

I made myself believe I loved him.

I made myself believe I never loved him.

I made myself believe he had power over me, and that was the worst lie I told myself, and the hardest one to break.

Fucking George. And if your name is George, I do apologize for bastardizing your name in this manner. I cannot explain how my ex-husband's name suddenly became George as I was writing my first book. I just knew that I needed to change it, and he is a vindictive asshole enough that if I even started with or had anything within the name that matched anything in his name, he would find a way of using it as a lawsuit against me.

Yes, he hates me that much. No he has never, and likely will never, own anything he has done. In his words, I am a "brainwashing bitch who lies," and he has never done anything to harm another person. Classic abuser lies.

I suppose it is suiting for me to insert an assurance here, perhaps in justification to myself, perhaps to assure you I am genuinely not a bitter-hearted bitch, but despite all evidence to the contrary, there is one part of my "situation" with George I cannot seem to let go of.

Spoilers: it isn't the anger, nor what was done to me or my children. In fact, I genuinely have forgiven him. There is a deeper lesson in how I am speaking about him throughout the pages of this book, a lesson that will come in time.

What I am unable to not hold within my heart is a sliver of hope. I have told David more times than I can count, "I don't have it in me to hold onto hope for George to change anymore. I gave him too many chances, and I have never seen anything to the contrary. It is always a sham."

Yet again, something I hold onto, perhaps unhealthily, is this one lie. I cannot keep hoping he will change. Yet, there is something that happened when David came into my life. I was shown and taught firsthand what a loving, dedicated father and husband is really like. A man from a hard background, in a city where he did not grow up, and was only here due to being stationed by the Air Force. He was married, had his son, and then was divorced.

By all accounts, the reference points I have of fathers does not involve staying in an area to be present in their child's life. No, even George waited until the divorce papers were signed and then he moved two hours away.

He could have stayed. The affair happened, he was remarried within months, but he chose to leave. Something he will never admit once more. Yet David came into my life and changed my whole perspective. With the shift came that little sliver of hope. It is truly one of the things within my heart holding an essence of purity.

I know the truth of who we all are on a soul level, and I always hope others will awaken to the truth of what they are doing to themselves and others, to their essence, their goodness, and heal. I hope, and simultaneously, I am real. I have seen too much, been through too much, and patterns cannot be discounted.

Abusers lie. They lie to others, they lie to the world, and they lie to themselves.

Truthfully, no matter how much an abuser is told they are harming someone else, they seem incapable of seeing it in that light. It is as though there is a grand fucking break in mental processing telling them everything they have done is justified.

Called into question from someone else, particularly from the person who they are continuing to hurt, well, it becomes someone else's fault. Painfully enough, it usually becomes the fault, in an abuser's eyes, of the person they are continuing to inflict trauma upon. They lack what is called emotional intelligence.

This isn't about being intelligent about emotions either. No, they know exactly how to play emotions off. They know how to make them bigger or applicable in order to create the illusion of it. It is a psychological illness due to a lack of empathy.

I am talking about the emotional intelligence we come to when we know, feel, allow for the fullness of the human emotional experience, and then choose to be a better human being.

Abuse victims are the ones who suffer the worst when they are trying to hold to an identity. No matter what identity they try to hold onto, it never works. They always end up with the wrong one. It is one of the harshest fucking truths I have had to face.

When I was with George, and even afterward when I was friends with Harry, when I welcomed a local family, the Pollumba's, into my home, all of these people I opened my life and my heart to, I was never going to be the right kind of person.

I was never going to be loved. I was always going to be exactly the kind of wrong person they needed in order to feed their very own egos. Honestly, the truth you should know at this point, and forgive me for saying this, in the spiritual community when we talk about people falling away from us, it is ridiculously passive.

Fuck, no. That isn't how it goes. When you are walking away from someone because your lives are no longer meant to be on the same path or whatever you want to call it, everything about yourself, your beliefs, and your identity suddenly are called into question.

You become the worst, most selfish person in the world for doing what is right for you. You are the bitch, the asshole, the narcissist.

God, even just talking about the way shit gets twisted by these kind of people makes me feel sick to my stomach. Most of the time, it made me not want to keep trying to speak my truth anymore. I didn't want to make friends. I didn't want to be a part of the world. I sure as fuck didn't want to be a part of the spiritual community as a whole any longer.

When did the few who are finding their bread-and-butter preying upon others within the spiritual community become the dominants?

I don't know, but I know a few of them by name (though I will not name them specifically here – and if you know me, you know the number one that always chaps my ass). I wonder how they are getting on with their millions of dollars for peddling fallacies through the world.

I don't have the heart or stomach to use fear-marketing, so I have found a hard time with sales.

How fucking sick is that?

This is one way we find a challenge to who we are. Are you going to engage in fear-marketing as a person in general? How about as a spiritual teacher? Psychic? Coach? Wife? Husband?

Are you going to choose to continue to be part of the mother fucking problem this world has or are you going to be the outlier and say, *Fuck all of that, I am going to work and move from my heart.*

Traditions be damned, I will not peddle fear in the world any longer. I want to see people get up on their soap boxes and take a stand against all the lies, propaganda, and fear-based sales and lifestyle. Just fucking burn that shit to the mother fucking ground (whoops, that isn't this chapter)!

As I was working through the editing process of this book, I have literally been consumed by its contents. Where once I would have expected it to be all the negative aspects one could attempt to find within these pages, in truth it has all been about the messages I am here to bring into greater awareness.

Last night I had a dream about fear-marketing (stay tuned for even more on this to come). I awoke and my left arm was completely numb. It was as though Professor Lockhart had tried to heal my arm and it suddenly had no bones. The left side, and in particular my left arm is my Divine Feminine energy indicator. It was numb. As though all the foundational bones had been completely removed.

In my head I was still seeing images and hearing myself say, "I will not use fear to find money. I will move from the heart, and it will matter." As soon as the words left my mouth in my dream, I felt my arm flood with feeling again. Our bodies are always our greatest source of information when we are learning what is and isn't right for us.

This world we live in has for too long had a very wounded Divine Masculine, coupled with a silenced Divine Feminine. Too long has this imbalance been here, too long has it led us all down a road and path we now must see and make the changes for.

We see this imbalance all the time, but for me I have seen it continually within the marketing industry. I have taken many courses and all of them seem to have the same formula. It matters not whether it is coming from the spiritual teachers or from someone who is a natural motivational speaker and has made their living inspiring others to live based on their techniques.

All fall into the same category: desires and fears bring in the money.

I had a long conversation with my mom a week or so ago. It was fraught with anxiety and financial stress, on my part, and her attempting to help me reason through finding some answer, some solution. She has watched me go on this journey, watched as my projects have taken off and then crashed, and listened to my pain, and anguish, and confusion as to why I am still trying to help others and make an impact in the world when it isn't helping me nor my family.

This is the side people don't talk about either. To the outside world, I know people perceive me as a success, yet my inner world is not allowing for that. My Divine Masculine needs more healing. A redefinition of what success really is. Yet, I know without a doubt that I am not the person to follow the system of *this is what works for everyone else so this is what we should all be doing*.

Truth is, if it worked for everyone and was what we were truly meant to be doing, there wouldn't be the imbalance in the world and especially in the financial world we are seeing and experiencing continually. This all boils down to how we believe we need to market to people.

Get them to sign up for a free session, then spend fifteen minutes in that hour talking about how they can take their personal freedom into their own hands, and it isn't that hard, and paint a rosy picture of distortion over the reality.

Well done, you have now played into the desires of these people. Now for the rest of the time talk about how if they invest their limited resources into you, you will promise they will never again hold themselves back and all their dreams will magically come true.

You play off their desires to hook them and then bait them with the fear they do not already contain within themselves the strength, brilliance, and resilience to make their dreams a reality. Put the icing of fuckery atop with, if you don't take advantage of this wonderful discount we are presenting to you during this limited time, you will never get this low of pricing again, you will never get these secrets, and you **NEED** their secrets to succeed.

How does this not make the majority sickened to see?

We are peddling nothing more or less than fear and expectations. If your system doesn't work, it becomes a failure of the person fighting for their dreams and not the system. We have been programmed and conditioned to not question the systems in place.

If we do not question them, if we do not ask *why the hell would I want to spread fear when I am trying to get my ass back to happy and out of fear*, how can a change ever occur?

Come the fuck on! It is high time for a change to be made here. Divine Masculine is not about peddling fear, it is about the actions taken that have been directed by the Divine Feminine. They work in tandem; they are meant to work in tandem.

All this means we must cease peddling fear like it is oxygen in this world and start fucking moving from the heart. It feels like a proverbial do or die moment. Right here, right now. What are you going to choose to do moving forward?

-3-

What is the other biggest challenge to who you are? I am genuinely curious about what it is you answer. For me, it was the person everyone else said I was. I was who I was needed to be for everyone else.

Since I was a kid, I was whatever other people needed me to be. I was the scapegoat. I was the black sheep. I was the sexual conquest. I was the throw away. I was the one who everyone loved to use, and no one loved. Sickening right? It isn't a lie; it was my fucking life. I have had to work my ass off to get the world to see me. To experience the kind of love I so easily give to others.

Who the fuck am I? Who the fuck are you?

Would you believe me if I told you at this point, I don't want an identity?

Where once that would have meant I was seeking only anonymity, now it is because I don't want to be labeled, boxed, or chained into one way of being. I even hesitate with calling myself an author, despite the fact I have two books published and am writing several more.

I cannot emphasize enough that I don't want an identity.

Let me be me.

Don't define me.

Don't label me.

Don't try to tell me who I am, and especially not if it has anything to do with what it is you want from me.

I built a healing program. Poured months of my time into writing it, and even more years into learning the fucking lessons I needed to learn in order to be able to write it in the first place. In the very first lesson it is all about this chapter.

I talk about what masks and hats we wear. Who we are for others. Who the world tells us we are. I do my best to help others to see they don't have to be labeled or defined. God, I have had to work my ass off to take my own god damn advice. Isn't that just the icing on top?

You know, I have sat here for days working on this, not knowing if it is meant to become something more than a plethora of pages of me bitching about everything that happened in my life. The thing about all of it is, when I think about gifting this to the public, I think about the carefully constructed persona I used to wear.

I think about the prim and proper way I would speak. The mouth of a sailor I use in this book, yeah, that is reserved for behind closed doors. My friends are aware, but my clients and my viewers and followers, not so much.

How utterly fucking duplicitous of me!

Should any of us then attempt to hold onto any semblance of our persona if it isn't the truest nature of who we are?

I have an even better one for you, one that is going to challenge you to your core. Why would it do that? Because it challenged me every time. I considered it right up until the day I said, *fuck it, I am going with it*, and the rest is history.

What if your persona was constantly changeable and you never had to explain to someone else why you seem different, you just fully own whatever persona you are any given moment?

FUCK!

Are you fucking kidding me? That would mean that you can change your emotions, you can swear, or you cannot, you can talk with your full vocabulary, or you can sling slang out of your mouth without a care of what other people think.

You could be every facet of your utterly multifaceted persona without explaining to anyone who you are, why you are behaving one way or another, AND continue to live your life how you dream of rather than worrying about Nosy Nancy down the street.

(If your name is Nancy, this is not a direct shot at you, unless you feel attacked and called out. As mentioned before, if you are offended, stop doing the thing I mention. Much love to you though, for real.)

Could life really be that freeing?

Could we truly live and let others live without requiring an explanation for why they are different?

Oh, don't worry, you may have forgotten the fact that I am a psychic. I also have suffered from abuse, trauma, and CPTSD/PTSD (yes, I am lucky enough to have experienced both), which inevitably means I know there are some situations in which this way of being is ridiculously dangerous.

Essentially what I am referring to are the moments in which George would shift gears in our marriage dependent upon who we were around. If we were around the people he wanted to impress or who he intended to be seen in an awfully specific light by, he would keep his attitude tempered and often good-natured while triggering me in order to make me appear unstable.

Clever little ploy don't you think? He still does that, and I don't try to call him out, I don't try to dictate one way or the other. His true nature is not for me to bring forth in his social circles, whether or not we are together.

All I do anymore, all you should ever do, is stand tall and tell the assholes doing this, "I will not take the responsibility for your emotions, actions, and behaviors. Your life is not mine. I take responsibility for my life. I do not accept yours."

After you say it, make damn sure you stand by that. You just put down a boundary, you owned your life and refused to accept another person's projection. Don't back down from your truth.

Everyone is entitled to the opportunity to make their own mistakes and learn their own lessons. Someone wants to believe that George is a victim of mine (and yes, this is his newest role he is playing at in public) as though he didn't beat me, as though his own children don't want to engage with him any longer because of his treatment of them, as though I have ever been violent toward anyone other than myself.

Seriously, if someone wants to believe that and enable a narcissist, frankly, they have to make that mistake. This was a bit of an excessive, and accusatory little snippet here, but it is highlighting my point.

Identities are kind of like the race and gender boxes on tax documents. You don't have to divulge the information, but if you do, you are labeled, grouped, and there is no getting out of it.

In an extreme, and albeit kind of terrible example, think about Michael Jackson. Checking one box, and then developing a condition in which that box simultaneously was and wasn't applicable.

Crisis city! Identities are constructs we hold onto when life becomes chaotic and messy because it makes us feel just a slight amount of control. The harder you hold to an identity that is a fallacy, the more the energy all around you is going to push you, bear down on you, and pressure you into changing.

When who we believed we are is called into question, it is in those moments we are experiencing a restructuring of our inner foundation. Don't fight it. Let it fall! Rome had to fall, and you know what, it is still in existence, it changed, transformed. You have the ability to do the same.

Our identities serve a purpose for the time we have them, but there comes a time in which growth becomes inevitable. Let yourself grow. Shed the layers upon layers of who the world tells you you need to be, or you are. Strip the masks of the roles you play in life. Spread your arms, look up to the sun, and tell Spirit you are ready to be you.

When I mentioned living and allowing others to do the same, I was hit with a plethora of people's thoughts. Every single one began with *What if...* and ended with some sort of challenge.

Whether you are one who engaged in it or not, here's the thing: you are fighting against something you have wanted for yourself because you don't want to allow another person who has wronged you to do the same. Fuck! No holds barred on that truth bomb huh? Now, you really should feel called out.

I was the same fucking way.

Do I want George or Harry to be able to run around and be whoever they want to be at any given point in time without explanation to anyone? Not particularly, no.

Why not? Because I don't want other people to get hurt. Because I was not afforded that opportunity by them, and because I can be a bitter selfish bitch at times. At least I will fucking own that aspect of me because she is me and needs love just like every other aspect of who I am. You see, this is the nature of the shadow aspects contained within us all. The parts within us we have rejected because of some situation or belief in the outside world. They are what we need to see, love, and realize we don't have to move from that place ever again.

What about you?

Could you do it?

Could you allow another person the freedom to change and grow like you are or have done?

Would you support someone being a better person if they said they were?

Would you watch someone change their persona as though changing clothes and NOT call them duplicitous?

It is a challenge for us to practice what we preach. Aligning our words with our actions. We have to learn, collectively how to accept the uniqueness of every other person we come into contact with. Some people aren't going to like you, some people aren't going to like me, you won't like some people, and I am fairly certain I have proven at this point there are people I don't like either.

Love and like are dramatically different notions. I do not have to like every person in the world to afford them the unconditional love that Spirit has taught me about. You do not have to like every person to give them love.

Love is not about holding onto a person either. It does not obligate you to keeping someone in your life. It does not require you to go out of your way to help them when it will cause you undue harm. That is not love. Love means allowing freedom. Allowing someone the chance to grow and change, but also the room to make mistakes and fall down. We all are here to learn and grow. We can help each other out, but if we are helping others to our detriment, no one wins in that scenario.

Who you are is not something meant to be definable, because whether you know it or not, you are expansive, unending, and undefinable. You and I both are the essence of pure love for we came from that love. We carry shadows and darkness within us. Pieces we are meant to love as well.

Every moment we are faced with asking ourselves who we are, what happened in our lives, and what we do from here, it is a pivotal challenge. This is a turning point for you, for me, and for society as a whole. We have to break ourselves free from the titles keeping us small, keeping us from being who we came to be, and from allowing others the same blessing.

Ugh, even I can feel the level of tension and challenge this is creating in others. You know what, that is perfect because it is going to lead us directly into...

Dissonance and Deconstruction

1

Dissonance, dissonance! Once upon a time, I hated dissonance. You know, sometimes I still do. Sometimes dissonance is the hardest pill to swallow. Yet I have learned a lot about dissonance. In particular the utterly transformative power it holds in all things, people, and places when it becomes overwhelming. I could go about defining what dissonance is but let me tell you a story instead.

I began studying Human Design after watching a YouTube video in which the creator mentioned it. She talks about being a Generator and how much this understanding changed her. I love anything and everything psychology. When mixed with esoteric and energy, which is my fucking jam! Yes, I am that badass!

I wanted to downplay the last statement, in fact, in the first draft of this book I did. As I worked through the editing process, I realized I was doing the same thing as always. I wouldn't be being true to myself if I were to say I don't think I am badass. No, that is something I am continually working on accepting within myself.

It is the sense of not wanting to be seen as egotistical, yet the rest of the world too often seems content with saying, "I am awesome. I am amazing," and they don't get challenged. Why should I challenge myself when I say that? Why should you?

Alright, for real though, I love these things so here I was expecting to love Human Design. And I did, for other people. NOT. FOR. MYSELF.

Do you remember way back in the opening pages, within Brutal Warning, where I mention the fact that if you are on the kind of healing journey I am on, you hit a point where your anger becomes directed at your own soul? Welcome to one of the worst offenses I have found my soul made against me! Fucking Human Design.

I am rereading a book right now that talks about how systems are keeping us in boxes. Systems feed into the illusion, the maya, the matrix. Perhaps, this is a system quite well designed, keeping us in a never-ending loop of "these are my restrictions." Or is it a test?

A test to see if we will swallow whatever someone else says and never try to work our own way through it. Tests in life are not just challenging, they are like an all-out bloody battle at times. This one, with the level of resistance I have to the system was one that left me wounded and on the sidelines.

Try as I may to discount the system, to cheat it, to disprove it, or to simply flat out not believe it, there are too many pieces of it which make perfect sense to me. We all can identify one system or another we want to break down and can't seem to find the fucking sledgehammer for. It sucks huh?

Yeah, I feel that in my fucking bones. We tend to fight hardest against the things that make the most sense. We fight because a lot of the time our logical mind will tell us what level of ludicrous these notions or beliefs or whatever are and our intuition will try to console us through the simple truth that if we found it, there is a reason.

Why don't I like human design?

Have you ever checked out your human design chart?

If you haven't, google it. There are a number of different sites that will give you a basic interpretation of it for free. Some have adapted it from the original system, some just give you the bare minimum with the intention to take you for hundreds or thousands of dollars.

If you don't want to do any of that, but you are keen on research, check out geneticmatrix.com. At least there you can do your own thing and find answers through your own methods and research rather than paying for someone else to tell you about yourself.

When I began doing *my* own research on Human Design, I used Genetic Matrix. I still do (though I have successfully moved away from being on the site every single day for hours on end). There is a section on there that shows the "Resonance Squares" which is a fancy way of explaining how your energy looks within the Human Design program dependent upon your astrological placements on the day you were born and on a day that happens to fall at 88 solar degrees prior to the day you were born.

Let's not get into the mathematical and calculatory issues I have found within this system, we are going to simply accept what it is they say for the fact that, yeah, a lot of it makes sense without me enjoying the fact it does. Fucking hell, don't you hate when there is a system so close to the edge of insanity, but it fucking resonates?! I fucking hate it!

Alright, let's get back to these "squares of bullshit" as I like to think of them. I haven't studied them fully, but I can see the screen and get the gist of it quite quickly. You know what I learned looking at those? According to the Human Design system, I am walking, talking, energetic dissonance in the world.

ARE YOU FUCKING KIDDING ME?

I am literally (according to Human Design) a walking change agent in the world. Maybe that sounds fun to you, but for me it means a lot of fucking discord in interactions and relationships. Supposedly, this is the source of why I don't make friends easily, and why I struggle to trust others (among the other reasons listed above).

Here is where I am opening myself up to a lot of attack from others. I know I am not an expert on Human Design, fuck, I don't know that anyone other than Ra can ever say they are a true-blue expert because it is so fucking out there of a system. With Ra being dead now, it is hard to definitively say anyone is an expert anymore. Oh well.

Why am I opening myself up to attack like this? Well first of all, not *all* my planets are utterly dissonant (it's like 85-90%). Secondly, I don't know the finer details of what it means per the Human Design system. What do I know?

Why the fuck am I talking about something that I openly admit I am not an expert on? Because I know myself, I know energy, and I know how it has presented in my life enough to stand here and tell you this fucking story.

Sheesh!

Why are we always such a challenging group of assholes?

And of course now you're likely to think, *I wasn't challenging the notion at all, you are losing it, you are getting defensive,* and so on and so forth. You are half right and half wrong. I can see the future and read energy.

Which inevitably means that I am picking up what my readers are going to respond with. Gotta say, this is the most interesting way I have ever written a book. This way of operating is usually reserved for when I do my tarot readings or when I do personal sessions, so you're welcome?

Alright, all bravado aside, because I know I sound like a stuck up, holier-than-thou brat when I am talking about my gifts, the real truth is that I am always at the mercy of whatever is going on energetically around me. It made learning about my own energy of paramount importance.

Learning about it left me sad, broken, and pissed beyond belief. I wasn't pissed at the Human Design system; I wasn't pissed at Ra for coming up with it. I wasn't pissed at Richard Rudd for breaking off and making a brutally honest explanation of genetics tied to this energy which fit my life too well. I don't blame anyone else; I wasn't pissed at anyone else. I was completely and utterly pissed at myself.

2

I have been livid with my own damn soul since learning about Human Design without being able to fucking bypass the system or change it, nor even worse change my mentality about it! When you already feel constantly dualistic, and yeah, we are all dualistic, you come to a point of asking yourself, "Do I really need to feel it and *see* it right in front of my face?"

Fuck no you don't!

This is what Human Design did to me, gave to me, whatever you want to call it. Essentially, the system showed me I was right about myself. Which means, in this very moment, I am going to choose to go back to the whole "I am a badass," quote. If my energy is complete and utter dissonance, and I am still able to have a happy, loving marriage and relationships, then I am fucking winning.

Am I just constantly repeating myself? I feel like I am constantly repeating myself. Fuck. Where did I lose my train? Maybe right around the area that "Shiny" from Moana got stuck in my head.

Listened to it and then all I was doing was going in the same circles in my mind. I haven't watched the movie in so long that I cannot tell you whether that is a sign, though some of you may be able to.

Where was I? Dissonance. Right. Okay, let's get away from me justifying using Human Design and find the fucking silver lining to all this bullshit, shall we? Maybe this is what "Shiny" was all about. The Human Design system is the shiny new system.

It is the new astrology, the new spiritual method. We all want something shiny that makes sense to us, but the shiny parts of things only serve to distract us.

We have to find the shadows, the silver lining, or diamond buried deep under the pressurized bullshit.

Alright, so starting off, I am going to tell you I am an Emotional Projector per my Human Design chart and that I have an open AND undefined Self Center. In the simplest terms with this, and I do mean simplest, the system asserts I learned about self-love and direction in life through other people as I don't really have a frame of reference for myself.

It also says I am designed to lead but not to do so by doing anything beyond telling others what to do, and I have to wait for people to recognize my own brilliance before I will matter in the world. Something along those lines.

Yes, I am paraphrasing and summarizing. Yes, there is a lot of sarcasm, and it is dripping with disdain in places. Yes, I am a bit more bitter than I would like to be because MY FUCKING SOUL chose this life. What the fuck was my soul thinking?!

What my soul was thinking is likely the same shit yours was whenever you find yourself in the midst of dissonance:

TIME FOR SOUL GROWTH BABY!

Because in all reality, the true reason for dissonance is not about showing us where we shouldn't be and who we shouldn't be around, it is in showing where we have some sort of internal issue we need to deal with.

Here is where I am going to deviate dramatically from many spiritual teachers.

Bear with me, it is going to be a bit of a wild ride.

Back in Noise Cancelling Bullshit, I talked about the background noise of the world. The opinions and beliefs of everyone else that tell you who you should be, what you should believe, what you are doing right, how you are wrong, whether you should love a person, and whether you should sacrifice everything for the notion of someone else who says they have all the answers.

These are just a few of the things that create heightened levels of dissonance in your energy field. They created heightened levels in mine as well, and as a person who is walking fucking dissonance, well here we have the issue really.

I was insecure about myself, which FYI, don't believe anyone who tells you they don't have any level of insecurities, they are fucking lying. It is always there like an undercurrent, but it is about overcoming it and knowing the truth of your worth.

I was taken advantage of easily by other people.

In particular this happened with spiritual teachers out in the world.

They would tout this belief or that belief, and the worst one was about relationships. If there is conflict, if one person is awakened and the other isn't, if there is hardship or whatever, let's constantly interpret it as the universe saying you have to leave the relationship you are in and choose a new one.

Okay, I get that there are cases in which this could be supported, but how fucking sickening is it to think that when you start a spiritual journey if your partner isn't of the exact same belief system as you, you aren't meant to be with them.

As though Spirit loving each one of us individually means nothing and we shouldn't love freely but should be far more selective about it.

3

Do we really understand what the premise of unconditional love is:

THERE ARE NO FUCKING CONDITIONS TO LOVING SOMEONE.

I paid someone to do a personal Tarot Reading for me once. She told me that my guides and spirit were telling me to forsake my heart, to walk away from love, and to be in my relationship would only bring more and more pain. What fucking audacity.

That was not what the message was at all. How do I know? Joys of being a psychic and choosing to own my life and my own power. Fucking hell, do you know how dangerous it is to just throw around words like that in this world.

The Spiritual Community has become a perpetrator in my opinion on this aspect. There is a difference between self-love and being utterly selfish. There is a difference between altruism and in-it-for-what-it-gives-me. Could be I am genuinely wired differently than the rest of the world, but I believe that love outweighs any and every belief and opinion of anyone and anything else in this world.

I believe we are built and made of love, we give and receive love, and we are meant to transcend all the lower-level bullshit into a state of unconditional, universal love. This does not equate with throwing away love because of the mindsets out in the world of the grass is greener all the time.

When did we stop fighting for the love we have and know we deserve being one in the same, but are willing to fight off anyone who says that we have to wear a mask in public or buy our way into heaven?

What the fuck happened to us all?

When did it get to this point?

I don't actually know how we have fallen so far from where we were on a soul level, but I do know we can all choose a new way of seeing ourselves and others and stop with all the bullshit.

I know this is going to garner a lot of flak for me, but it is high time to get rid of the ridiculous notion of Twin Flames.

Just stop.

You know I say this, despite the fact I believe in them myself. I also see how toxic the idea is. I see the lie of them. I see the way it breaks families apart, tortures people, and makes the crazy come out when one believes or knows they have found their Twin Flame.

Twin Flame in the 2020s is much the same as Soul Mates in the 2000s. New name to make a relationship more special. If you need a fucking label to make your relationship special, it isn't a special relationship.

See there I go spewing my personal opinion about things. I have been the teenager that called boyfriends soulmates like it meant something super special. We made it, as a society, into something to be revered until it was overused, and then it was just a whatever. We have multiple soulmates, and they can range from animals to children to love interests to friends to your fourth cousin twice removed on your father's side.

Soulmates are just another word now for the friendships and connections we have in life. I still remember the time that soul mate was tantamount to destined love of all time. Now that is known as Twin Flames.

Whenever we are struggling within ourselves or struggling within a relationship, we will glom onto these beautified notions of titles for the person we are with. David is my soulmate. He is my twin flame. He is my best friend. He is my husband.

Why do any of those things matter more than the fact that he is the man I love?

Spoilers: they don't.

None of the titles matter more than what the heart feels.

We have forgotten how to hear the heart over the din of the mind and the background noise of the world.

What does the heart even sound like? Queue the sarcasm of, well it sounds like a thumping, it beats, it's a thud-thud-thud. I always expect the sarcastic, dad joke-esque comments because, well, David.

On a logical level, sure, it sounds like a beating.

On an emotional level, what your heart sounds like, shit, it is something you have to train yourself to hear. You have to learn to move from a place that holds no words, but all the power and emotions. This is how you have to listen. It isn't just about listening either. We all need to learn to hear our hearts. Hearing and trusting. It will be different for you than it is for me. It isn't something that can really be taught, only discussed.

And on that note, I am telling you right here and now, do not ever let someone tell you they are going to teach you to listen to your heart. That is their minds telling you the fallacy of the beliefs they have. Your heart will never listen to another person, it will only speak to you.

There are too many of us out here now. Too many awakened and too many that are learning the gentle voice of the heart. It cannot be negated or taken advantage of anymore.

This is something we are seeing with Evangelicalism, with Christianity, and with most religions. The more there are awakened souls, the less the old ways will hold any power and impact. The less that exists, the greater the need for deconstruction of thoughts, beliefs, and behaviors throughout the world when there is dissonance that arises.

We have begun shifting now from a phase of deconstructing organized religion, governmental structures, the monetary system, and more and soon enough, sooner than we realize for it truly has already begun, it is spirituality which will be deconstructed.

All these things I am saying, they are predictions, observations, and channeled information. If they don't match with you, you aren't ready to hear this, you aren't on the same timeline, whatever the argument, it matters not. All of the resistance you likely feel toward me and/or this message has to do with the dissonance you are feeling within. It is about being fearful of challenging the systems in place, the ones needing an overhaul.

If you are where I am, let's deconstruct every last fucking notion until the only thing that remains is the ever-pervasive truth of everything: **LOVE**.

Magic and Mayhem

1

Be fucking careful when you ask for a miracle. I have said it before, I will again, I am not going to sugarcoat any of this shit. I will make you a promise right here and now, and I do not make promises that I cannot keep – what I am telling you, it is not a lie. It is not a fabrication. This shit fucking happened; it was my fucking experience. I am sitting here writing about all of this shit, because it is time to speak out about it.

I would love for this to be a frilly section about miracles and rainbows. I mean, I am fairly certain I have mentioned that a few times now. I truly do wish it were like that. This section is about the unshed blood from the wounds inflicted during an experience which took months passing for me to realize I had predicted for myself, and still yet wasn't fully prepared for.

This is where we are going to drive directly off the cliff of anything and everything resembling sanity and dive straight down into the mythical and magical ways in which we learn lessons. This lesson for me was about learning to heed my heart, learning to listen to myself, and learning to walk away from situations and people that were not right for me.

Ironic isn't it after the chapter we just had and me defending the choice to remain in relationships despite what others said, I would open this one with the bitter recall of the relationships I was not meant to be in. This time the warning and message was coming from within.

By all outside accounts, I should have maintained these connections and friendships. it was my intuition and inner landscape telling me to run the fuck away, screaming about the danger of the situation and the need to be anywhere else except the friendships I was in during this time.

Let's time travel again, shall we? This time we are going back to the fall of 2021. Scorpio, Sagittarius into Capricorn season. Those happened to be my fourth, fifth, and sixth houses in my natal chart, and the ones that pack the biggest punch of outer planets.

There is nothing but transformation imbued in my personal energy during that time of the year. I am talking end of October through mid to end of January every year. When my life has a new way of being, a new adjustment, and new depths open up.

I could continue to break down the astrology of all of it, but that isn't for this book. The reason I bring it up is because of the timing of everything, and the awareness of just what depths of energy I was dealing with.

If you are someone who knows astrology, then you know having Scorpio as the ruler of my Imum Colei and my fourth house coupled with my Pluto being in Scorpio is potent on its own. Add with Mars in Cancer in the 12th, and Cancer being my sun sign. If you love astrology as I do, then you will see and understand almost instantly just what magnitude of "holy shit" deep inner transformation and ancestral karma my whole nature is, and that time was no different.

Have I made enough foreboding, foreshadowing allusions of mystery yet? I could keep going, but instead I am going to tell you a quote from my dreams/visions journal and then we are going to talk about November 11, 2021 – and the three days of torture, confusion, and "miracles" that I experienced. It is going to sound a lot like a fantasy, an illusion, or a drug induced trip.

I can tell you with all assurances, though there were several people involved, I was the one who felt it all.

I was the one who suffered.

I was one of the only ones, if not the only one, who was never once under the influence of any drug or alcohol. It is important to me for you to understand that this is not a typical spiritual "herbal" trip. This is me, my life, and part of what I endured.

One more caveat for you all – I don't have an explanation to this day. I believe for the rest of my life I am going to perpetually wonder about those three nights, wonder about the experience. Wonder what was going on, why I experienced it, what the point of it all was, and whether it was real or not.

My intuition is telling me it was all real and it led me here so that is answer enough. My logical mind is telling my intuitive mind to shut the fuck up if it doesn't have some sort of concrete evidence to provide me with.

See, dissonance, even internally. Never really stops, you just have to transcend it.

I told you all I had gotten myself involved with an online community based on a program developed by two spiritual teachers.

Because of the discord with actions and behaviors, I am no longer involved in the community, nor can I access the program. This isn't because of any wrongdoing from the creators, it is because my energetic alarm system will not allow me to get involved with it any further.

Before I had developed this "alarm system," and before I learned how to hear myself and know myself, I found myself allowing an openness to new people, including those within the community. I would love to be able to sit here and say this was a massive mistake, but it wasn't.

It needed to happen.

Ugh, I hate that. I do. I don't like telling you I know a trauma I endured needed to happen. If you don't believe that for your life, please don't take what I say as your ultimate truth either. Know you first.

Within this community I met a few people. It was like lightning striking when we all came together. The energy of all of us within the same group was nothing more or less than supercharged hurricane force winds whipping around. It was destruction on a cellular level. Destruction on a physical, mental, and emotional level.

It was exciting and exhilarating. At the same time, it was terrifying, and nearly led to my downfall in life. I still am amazed in a way that I survived it.

On August 5, 2021, I had laid down to take a nap. As I was awakening from sleep, images were still flying through my third eye. As I opened my eyes, I looked at my right foot, and had a welt on top of the foot. I had been meticulous about journaling my experiences over the last couple of years. This was no difference. I am going to show you what it was that I channeled.

"Right now, the word I can hear in my head is Stigmata, there was a mark on my right foot in the middle on top in the dream and another, but it is hazy on its location, but as I write this there is a right side, back flank stabbing sensations, which is the approximate locations of the spear pierce to Jesus as well.

I also felt instantly called to listen to 528 HZ which is the heart chakra, but the playlist is called Repairs DNA and Brings Positive Transformation."

Channeled Message:

"The pain of the son is felt in the father. All pains experienced are never experienced alone, whether awakened or sleeping yet, our connection to the Divine Creator is eternal, and through this, take comfort knowing each pain has too been endured by the one who brought our souls into existence. He/She (there truly is no sense in gender assignment beyond what you feel you need in this life) is the eternal, immortal essence of love, patience, trust, and compassion, yet has endured all the suffering we too endured, and that of your loved ones, your friends, your enemies.

What we experience, so too does the Divine Creator, what the Divine Creator pours out is not, never has been, and never will be pain, but rather the purity, cleansing, healing unconditional love we all seek, not realizing it is already within ourselves. Asking and patiently waiting for us to return home to ourselves, our hearts, our compassion. To sit in this space within and to observe the changes and feelings washing over, through, and out of us as Divine Love rushes through us all.

What beauty there is, hidden inside, spreading out in a beautiful web of love, guidance, synchronicity, and safety. Go within and allow for love to wash you clean from the old perception that you have ever walked alone."

*Footprints: "It was then that I carried you."

_____

2

I honestly didn't remember the visions, the physical manifestation, nor the message. I had forgotten it until about two weeks prior to starting to write this book. This isn't unusual, honestly. When I sit down and channel like this, I do not often remember what I am channeling.

I know and trust that when it is time for me to realize what it was fully and consciously, then I will be brought back to it and move forward from there. Why I was brought back recently, well it makes sense to me now, for I am sitting here finally ready to open up about these experiences.

It was three months and four days later when shit hit the fan. It wasn't even like I enjoy saying, hitting the proverbial fan, no, there was fucking shit flying everywhere. It all started on November 9, 2021.

Are you sitting here and wondering what it was that started?

Would you believe it was exactly the word I was hearing after that dream vision back in August?

Yep, I fucking experienced stigmata.

Do I wish that I were lying?

Yes and no.

First of all, why the fuck would anyone ever lie about something like this, I don't know. I don't see it as being something special I endured. I don't know why someone would want it to happen either. The only real reason I have the feeling of wishing I were lying or rather over-exaggerating is because no one wants to experience this level of pain and anguish, this confusion and torture.

This is why I say, be careful what you wish for. When you ask for a miracle, be careful what it is you ask for or rather make sure you are incredibly specific. This was something that was absolutely a miracle, and I had for months been asking and begging for miracles. I wasn't specific, and the miracle was not what I bargained for.

I attempted to go to my glib, sarcastic nature when I was on the phone with my mom after the whole experience. "You know, I think next time I consider asking for a miracle, I am going to be incredibly detailed. Be careful what you wish for."

For three days straight, in particular at night, I would experience pains in my back as though I was being whipped. I would cry out in anguish, my muscles jerking on their own as though I was in and out of my body simultaneously. My head was killing me, my legs wouldn't work, and I could feel more pain and anguish than I could have ever imagined in my life.

The program that founded the community where this all started, ran a three-day promo. For three days, the founders were pumping everyone up about how to turn spiritual gifts and dreams into a full-time job.

Telling these magnificent stories. Well-polished, perfectly structured to empower others through hope, and then using fear to reel everyone in. Fuck was I ever naïve about fear marketing at this time.

Looking back now, I can see I really should have slowed myself down and allowed myself to listen to my guides, but that isn't what I did. I also should have taken my own personal guidance and taken the opportunity to wait and listen to my heart. I didn't do that either.

What I did was listen to two people outside of myself who were seemingly more successful. Yet, the measure of success for me back then was all about money. It was about financial abundance, the home, the car, the clothes, all the bullshit that doesn't matter but would be fantastic to have. No, in truth, neither of them were more successful than I, they were successful in their own way, but so was and am I.

So are you. That is one area we will discuss after all of this, how you see success. It is deeply important for you to know that when you are manifesting miracles, when you are working with other people, when you are joining something, you need to know yourself.

You need to trust yourself.

You need to understand yourself.

Fuck, you need to not hear anyone else other than yourself and your connection to your higher self and Spirit. Never fucking doubt that part.

There I was, sucked in. I began to become completely consumed by being a part of a community, finding the people who think, feel, and live like I do. I was consumed, and my family began to suffer. I began to suffer. My marriage began to suffer.

I was back in the wounded empath role, taking care of everyone over myself.

And I was like a beacon to these people. I was always working to help others, to love and light the fuck out of people in a negative situation. It was making me sick. Literally and figuratively.

3

Right as I was about to break away from it, I received an email about the monthly zoom coaching call. I jumped on in the hope it would be what I needed. Strangely enough it was and wasn't at the same time. It brought into my life people that needed to come in and set me upon my path even further, but they were not to be the people who would help me in a good way.

No, it was to be painful, delusional, and crazy making. Not only for myself, but for all of us. Some of us have not come back from the crazy portion of it.

There are two in particular who are still in the delusion of that time, that space. Two others are going about their lives, both still lost, both hurt, but I know they will grow and become better and more than they are right now and would have been in our group. And then there is me, the fifth.

The elected leader, the used and then strong one who was attacked, abandoned, and the one who broke away from the others as well.

Funny isn't it.

We all do what we have had done to us.

It is about how we go about doing it to others. When I experienced abandonment in my life, it was something that came with a beating, and being told how worthless and unlovable I am.

All the worst words, the most painful actions that could be taken short of killing me (though there certainly were some moments in which George genuinely did try to kill me – spoilers, he failed), those were my experiences. When I abandoned others, I tried not to lash out. I tried to not hurt them. I tried to do it without vengeful actions. I was not always successful, but I did genuinely try.

Why we all split apart started with stigmata. It grew into jealousy and envy, labels and titles, fallacies, and serious delusions. It then turned into a breakdown of what I believed would be the beginning of the greatest phase of my life.

I had a vision, each one of these people were part of this vision. When it was all said and over, there was no future left to gaze into, and I had no idea what was left for me to do.

Did you know that Jesus broke his nose when he carried the cross?

Did you know that he felt alone and abandoned, hated, and scorned?

Did you know he doubted himself and his path?

Did you know he was a father?

Did you know he was in love and abandoned his family and his love for the sake of other people?

Did you know that he was made to suffer, and it was amplified because he was a witch and an empath and a psychic and a yogi and a mystic?

Did you know that Jesus felt the emotional pains of the people all around him and throughout the world in a very physical way?

Did you know that the physical torture he experienced was minor in comparison with the emotional and mental transmutation he engaged with for others?

These are all things I learned, and saw, and experienced over the course of three days from 11/9/2021 until 11/11/2021. I am a numerologist; I am also a psychic and spiritualist. The 11/11 portal with the 5 year of 2021 was the most potent and powerful leadership change the world has seen in years.

I went through that portal in one way. My friends went through it dramatically differently.

The things I was shown, the titles I mention in the questions above, all of it were about perception. It was a challenge within, aimed at my conditioned mind for what titles really mean to me personally. All those questions are truth or fallacies, either one you choose is simply a label, a box. It was about the prospect of seeing outside of what everything in the world says is the truth. It was a lesson about what we accept as truth, what we are shown, and whether we are going to trust the images from Spirit without proof versus the words of humans.

You see, something I had to learn is to transcend the fear surrounding my truth being in direct contradiction with my religious upbringing. It was about seeing through to find what matters. My greatest lesson was for me to learn my truth is for me, and only when I choose to bring it to the world with purpose and clarity is there anything to consider. If Spirit/the Universe/God/etc. gifts you with insights and they challenge what you thought you knew, give yourself time to sit with it, mull it over, and find the deeper purpose.

It is neither my fault nor theirs, the delusions, the experiences. We all had our own, in our own way. We all saw one thing from our individual perspective. We were in the tides of crazy making thoughts swirling around, pure chaos, yet back then, there were two people who would tell you without a doubt they watched me experience Jesus's crucifixion as Jesus himself.

You would have several people tell you they believe I am Jesus reincarnated. Hell, during that time I would have said the same thing, albeit with an added exasperated, "Not that I would even want that. Who the hell would want that?" I wouldn't say that now, I don't believe it for a second. I needed to learn more, and I have.

---

*Of note:** I have realized here, I really haven't spoken much about the actual experience. The way one night I suddenly developed severe drop foot in my right foot. I couldn't walk, and tripped. Falling to the floor, bruises forming on my knee, my ankle throbbing, and my leg bleeding. There were small indents in the skin on the palms of both my hands as they throbbed mercilessly.

The jerking of my body as my back spasmed in pain I have no descriptive words for. How David's eyes filled not with doubt but rather with sheer panic at what I was experiencing. I was sobbing and crying in pain, and he asked, "What do we do to stop this?"

I knew in that moment the exact answer, "Nothing. I have to ride this out. It will pass."

He was so angry. It was every level of rage at everything invisible causing me pain. There was no logic behind any of this, it was merely energetic pain. Looking back now, it is like an illusion. I am not convinced I knew what was going on. I do know I felt something within my heart chakra I had never before felt. It was as though my chest were being ripped open, edges jagged, and the hopelessness and pains of the entire world were being poured through me.

My face in the pillow, I found myself screaming. I wanted it to end. I wanted to end. Like fiery lava of emotional pain and anguish was consuming my entire being, and I was powerless. All I could do was cry and mentally beg for help, beg for strength, beg for it to end.

It's a funny thing that happens when you are told someone else reading your energy has interpreted you as Jesus Reincarnated and told you, you have the power to create and destroy Universes. I think a lot of people would become crazed with power. In fact that is what the woman who read my energy, Judy, became.

Judy and Harry became obsessed with who they are, who their Higher Selves are. They became hyper focused, and I blindly agreed and encouraged it. I was so caught up in the drama and manipulation and not wanting to be alone that I didn't listen to me, I let others dictate.

I can tell you definitively that I am not Jesus reincarnated, that God is not my higher self, that Archangel

Michael is not incarnated in physical form, and that Shiva is not a woman in America who is the daughter of a Preacher Man. I can tell you these things because they were all part of the delusion.

This is what brainwashing looks like firsthand. I cannot quite explain away the physical experience of it all, nor what started it or ended it. It was what needed to be, a fact I simply have no other option but to fully embrace and accept. Yet, there was something more that felt as though it was going on. A viscous background noise in the group that felt every level of wrong.

Looking back now, it is hard to find a clear thread of what happened. Everything melded together. I thought I was the leader when really it was someone else working to manipulate us all. A woman I trusted who took something I built in order for her to try to make money and a name off of it. Fraud and deception blended together with my desire for connection, bringing to light an inner healing well overdue.

So many lessons came from living through being whipped, through the suffering of the world, feeling as though I was Pandora, opening the box, consumed by pain. Tormented and tortured, feeling nails in my hands and feet, and blood that wasn't there trickling down my head and face from my broken nose and cuts, or Jesus's broken nose which felt like it was mine.

What a fucking way of trying to describe something I feel like I haven't really described at all.

That is how it goes though isn't it? We think things are meant to be explained in a specific order and detail, we think that is how life is meant to be, but it isn't linear, it is chaos. This whole section has been the chaos of what happened.

Everything happened and nothing happened. It was and it wasn't. It was a time of the purity of living and experiencing a physical manifestation of the Law of Polarity, the truth that for every experience there is a lack thereof . For every up there is a down, for what occurs above, occurs below.

I would have died. I should have died. I could have died.

I might have stopped breathing if it weren't for the three people who experienced that reenacted journey of Jesus with me. I might have lost my mind. I may have really lost all sanity.

You see, they aren't terrible people. They are wonderful people to whom I tried to open up. People who lied to say what they needed to in order to take from me for themselves because they fail to see their own worth.

People who were there for me during something I couldn't make sense of but when they realized they wanted to experience something similar elected to lie and distort themselves, and the truth. When I chose to hold my truth back right away, it was fuel for their actions.

Don't hold your fucking truth back.

Don't do it.

Don't.

-4-

It matters not what you need to say, nor the fear of your truth being received poorly by others when holding something in which is meant to be out in the world is beginning to destroy you and your life. Don't fucking do it anymore. I cannot emphasize enough how much you should be yourself, how much your truth needs to be spoken.

Don't make assumptions. They make you an ass and I won't have you making one out of me. When you do this, you hold back your own personal freedom, trapping yourself within your own negative mindset. If you choose to speak, do it without the intention to be retaliatory.

Don't call people out directly. Speak from the heart and have a clear purpose for what you want the world to know. This requires you to have learned the lessons, given yourself forgiveness, and forgiving any and all who may have been involved.

This is decorum. I am telling you all of this because for some of you, your guide team just popped into my space. My ears began ringing and they want you to learn something valuable right here and now.

I cannot tell you what the lesson is. I know I am being vague beyond belief, but this is the way that channeling works. I don't always know what it is I am sharing, but I know and trust right in the moment, you need to read this, hear this, and you will know exactly what it is.

For Harry, as I know you will be reading this because I can see it in my third eye: I choose to forgive you. I don't care if you feel I am the one who owes you an apology. I don't care if you think you have undertaken actions that are beyond reproach.

I don't care how you view things, because I know when you are caught in the shadows, when all of us are caught in the shadows, we don't see anything clearly enough, and we hurt people horribly bad. I didn't take my actions from a shadow state, I took my actions because my guides led me to doing so.

I hold no ill will towards you, I forgive you, and I choose for you and for Judy to absolve you both from any incurred ties and debt. If the Universe so wills it.

Why did I do something so personal in a book that I am releasing to the world? Because it was a lesson as well. The words I shared, the intention behind them, were just as much for Harry and Judy as they were for me. This is something you can do for yourself. Whoever it is who hurt you in the past, let yourself free from the old you, let them free from that way of being. This is how you move on. Give forgiveness, say it purposefully, and mean it. Then walk away and think no longer on it.

We went through hell together. It was our own version of war. And we all had to go our separate ways. Some of us hurt the others horribly bad. Some of us took from the others and set out to prove the others wrong. For two of us, we just wanted to return to our lives, and find peace, calm, purpose, happiness, and a way forward.

That is what we all deserve in this life. What we want, what our souls want. I don't know why my soul chose to experience the crucifixion in this way. I do know it brought me closer to my mother, my brother, and my sister-in-law. It bridged the chasm between me and David, for when it was over and I looked in his eyes, I was able to truly see how we are one in the same. It helped me to let go of my fear about organized religion and refocus on my spiritual path and purpose.

I told you earlier in this book, the lesson of the Universal Law of Oneness was slammed into me in the form of torture.

This was how I was able to truly see just how connected everyone and everything is. Just how much we are all one, all with the same purpose: Love.

I was shown how each one of us is uniquely individual, uniquely gifted, uniquely our own self, while being made and sourced in love, unconditional, deeper than the oceanic abyss, love.

It taught me the value of loving myself and what sacrifice brings. It showed me the safety in making a different choice for myself and living for me, and the people, and things that are important to me rather than endeavoring to save the world.

Sometimes we have to endure torture in order to learn things like intent, purpose, and self-worth.

We have to suffer in order to stop self-sabotaging. Not every lesson is going to be full of magic. Sometimes it will be mayhem. Sometimes the pain will outweigh everything else, and all you will know to do is sit down, and cry, and beg Spirit to tell you why and what you are meant to do.

In order to transcend suffering, trauma, abuse, and the shadow state we have been living in for far too long, we first must understand it intimately. This is why there is still suffering in the world. We are in a perpetual learning state. Until the whole of the collective can come to understand the suffering is meant to teach of the polarity, just as fear is meant to teach of love, we cannot completely transcend.

It takes not one, but all. We all must learn these lessons. Therefore, there will always be those like myself who are here, who awaken, who speak out through our own unique filters, all with the same purpose and intention. To bring awareness back to the self, the connection to Spirit, and the way we are meant to truly be, the way we truly are.

When it was all said and done, I lost all sense of what I wanted in my life. After deep inner healing, I found myself right back to where I am right now.

Wanting to do the things that fill me with happiness and wanting the people in my life who love me for me and not for who they want me to be or who I can be for them.

You can take this opportunity to learn from me, to overcome what I couldn't, before you find yourself missing everything you once believed you would have.

Measuring Success

Do you have kids? I do. One thing I maintain while simultaneously struggle to break free from is wishing more for my children than what I had. Let me explain. We measure success in society with a fucking money ruler.

It is about status and privilege, money in the bank, and what *things* we have. This is a deep conditioned belief that spans across all ages. I already mentioned the fact I had to come to a truth within myself, I was being led by the words of others due to seeing them as more successful than I. All because they made money from doing what it is they love. How fucking sick is that?

This system of measurement is the reason why the world is in chaos and economic turmoil all the time. The rich have to maintain their wealth. They no longer consider giving it to others or sharing. They continue to stockpile it as though money will be there in the darkest of times. More deluded of a notion is one seemingly seeping through time from the Ancient Egyptians, in that if we are buried with our jewels or with our money, we will take it with us when we go.

Folks! Have we not already covered how life and death works? We come in alone, we go out alone. We take with us into this world only one thing, and it is the exact same as when we exit it: our soul. Money is not here to be something we grasp tightly to, chase after, nor hate. Money is here as energy. It is meant to bring balance into the things we exchange between each other. Yet it is not balanced in the world, a fact that can no longer be denied.

Because of this ridiculous imbalance, those like me, like you, like most of the general population, struggle to make some sort of mark of progress financially. When we hit a certain point, we see ourselves in a better light.

This is why I hate that the saying, "Money makes the world go round" is true, in notion.

What if it wasn't though?

What would happen if the rich would see the lifestyle they live isn't worth it?

What if those rich and famous settled for living in a house that wasn't big enough to house a third world country's population, but instead lived in a house that had enough rooms for the people who were in the family along with maybe one or two guest rooms and an office or something?

Would they still be a television or movie star?

Would they still be a world-famous singer or producer?

Of fucking course they would.

Would you still be you if you had more money or less money?

Yes, you would.

If you don't like who you are, change it. Don't change who you are because you want to attain some level of monetary success, do it because you want to be a better person. Money is energy, it is not a mark of success, esteem, or worth. Until we cease to see ourselves through the lens of our bank accounts, what we are able to purchase, and who we are showing up as in the world, this major imbalance remains.

-2-

Are you all sick of me talking about George? That's alright, he just is such perfect source material for a compare and contrast situation. I could present it as him being someone else, but herein lies another lesson. We interact with people for a long time, and when we do so, we learn a lot about ourselves.

George taught me a lot about myself by the suppositions he would make about my worth outside of the marriage. I either needed to make money, and then what I made needed to be spent on him, or I couldn't work because I was the wife and mother, and it was expected of me to clean and tend to the house and care for the children.

There was no in between.

Neither one made me successful, they were both a mark of some sort of failure.

Because of this, coupled with growing up with little to no money, little to no financial support as a child, I was, I suppose you could say financially handicapped. If you feel offended by that statement, please never go golfing because I also use a handicap in golf.

GET OFF IT PEOPLE!

Ugh!

There is something that bothers the fuck out of me, and this is a bitch fest is it not? We have to mince our words. Our tongues permanently walking on eggshells because there is always someone who is going to misinterpret something said as being offensive.

Fucking hell. I don't like the whole prospect of "Snowflakes" but in a lot of these situations, these are people who are bitching to hear the sound of their own voices and not because they have something important to say.

Don't waste a beautiful throat chakra and soul mission by spouting off bullshit you don't mean and won't own up to saying in ten years' time, do something fucking different please.

Alright, tangent done and onto the mistakes we make as parents, because as a parent I can certainly tell you we make a great many of them.

Today's parental mistake is brought to you by the notion of success!

Why do we wish more for our children than that which we had?

Because we want to live vicariously through our children rather than allowing them to be their own person?

Fuck!

Truth bombs are flying here.

This was another lesson that came in multiple ways over the course of many years. It started with George and his blind belief that our children should behave and believe as he says they should. Not how he does, but how he says they should. To him, they are pawns, his property, and as such must reflect the illusion of perfection he wishes for the world to see.

This is an important distinction that needs to be made. Not for the sake of George, but for the sake of you realizing whether or not you are the same way. I most definitely subscribed to the "do as I say and not as I do," parenting tactics. Part of the warrior arising within me, that came when George made it clear his belief the children were his property and not their own people.

I could blame George for the former. I could say it was during our marriage, I was a specific way as a parent, and then I changed dramatically after. That is absolutely the truth. It isn't his fault though.

Nope.

Sorry guys.

If you resonate with this then I am sorry to have to tell you that straight up, it is 100% on your shoulders.

Welcome to the reality of adulthood. We need to learn how to take ownership of our actions. When we measure what we view as success we need to see that our measurements are likely skewed because of the way that we were raised, and our parents were raised, and their parents were raised, and so on and so forth.

Fucking hell, the only way to stop this from continuing is for you to realize the truth and make a fucking change.

If infidelity runs in your family, learn to say no to a relationship until you are completely committed, and your little Johnson or Virginia isn't ready to go wandering from person to person to make you feel better. If alcoholism runs in your family, find a new past time other than the bar scene. Make trivia and physical exercise cool if your family doesn't read or work out and has a long running tendency to sit in front of the television and eat junk food.

If your parents told you, they wanted this or that for you all because they didn't have it:

DO NOT PUT THAT PRESSURE ON YOUR CHILDREN.

How fucking unreasonable is the notion that success unfound in one life can be made up through our children! What level of pressure they must feel from us for these things we place upon their shoulders!

I am not perfect in any sense with this. Of course I want more for my children than what I grew up having. Yet, if I were to make them live up to the things I felt as though I couldn't live up to myself, it makes me hypocritical, and places unrealistic, bordering on cruel, expectations on their shoulders.

If I want my children to have more than what I had in my life, if you want yours to have more, then show them how to have more by fighting for your own fucking dreams, and wishes, and goals.

I am sitting here, a few months away from turning 35, and I haven't finished college. There are so many things I haven't done, but I am writing my third book. I have embraced myself and built courses, owned my psychic and spiritual gifts, and am building a business from the ground up. I have done all these things my parents never did. They didn't but these are what I want for myself.

Have you heard the saying, "Be the change you want to see in the world"?

Who said that anyway?

I need to google it.

Give me a moment.

Well, I feel a bit like an idiot. Were you groaning and screaming at me that it was Ghandi? Or did you have to look it up too because it has become so fucking common place that we have all lost sight of what the actual message wrapped in these words really is about? My money is on the second one. It's alright, no judgement. I am the same way.

Good ol' Ghandi. Teaching forever. Never stopping the lessons, but man, he has got to be sick to death of all us idiots down here choosing to spout off his words to others, but not actually live true to them. Be the change you want to see in the world. Change your inner world first because there is where true, lasting change in your outer world will be found. And for all those "progressive" types who want to invalidate any person we might learn lessons from because of mistakes they made in their lives, remember that you too may be remembered forever, and if you require absolute perfection from others, you have to hold yourself to the exact same standard.

There is no genuine compare and contrast in this matter. Everyone makes mistakes. Some are on a far greater scale than others, but we all make them. This is something driving me bonkers in the world. Everyone thinks because they can google the actions someone has taken they should discount the good they did. Are you Ma'at? Are you able to justifiably weigh a person's heart against a feather? Would your heart be that light?

If you answer no to any of those questions, it is time for you to stop bitching about the teachers that came before and choose to become the teacher you believe they should have been. Be the fucking change you want to see in the world rather than sitting back and complaining continually about all the wrong doings of people from the past. Do it differently. Do it better. Be the fucking change.

Let's think about this in terms of success, shall we?

-3-

How can you be the change you wish to see in the world with your perspective and parenting? First of all, you need to know what the fuck you want for yourself.

Seriously, this might be one of the harder tasks for you to figure out. We all think we know what we want. It oftentimes is something we didn't want, but rather something we wanted to attain or achieve in order to make someone else happy.

What do you want? What is it that you want for yourself so badly that you wish your children would have it and more?

That!

THAT RIGHT THERE!

It was the first thing that popped into your head, and then you passed it off like it wasn't something important.

THAT IS WHAT YOU ARE HERE TO DO!

Can it really be so easy? Of course it can! We are programmed (and I use that lightly because too many people are caught up in the notion of the matrix without fully understanding what it actually is), or conditioned, to believe we are here for something other than what we really are.

We think of that first thing, but we have trained ourselves to stop thinking about it, to forget about it, to believe it isn't right or possible, so we push it into the back of our minds and become tortured every fucking day.

For me, I am going to tell you honestly, my first thought is *I want to be a New York Times Bestseller.* After publishing two books and realizing how averse I am to the marketing realm, watching the slow trickle of sales unless offered for free, I worked my ass off running in the opposite direction. It brought me to right before the stigmata bullshit.

Oh! Epiphany moment! Wow, you guys are lucky. I am going to share with all of you how things can just fall into our awareness and understanding when we release the constant chase to define it. When I published my books, the first thing I did was start brainstorming ideas for the third book. I had a plan. I knew what it was I wanted, and I was going to keep going.

At the same time, I was taking on too many different projects, not allowing myself to believe in my writing. I went running scared because of my definition of success. One book selling to a complete stranger should have marked success for me. A fucking published book in my hand, that should have been my marker. It wasn't.

I was consumed by the time I had spent, the money I had spent, and the blind hope and faith I would do all this work and be an overnight success. We live in an instant gratification world, and it seriously cripples our patience and growth.

I was definitely victimizing myself with this way of thinking.

I began a negative biofeedback loop of thinking: *I didn't have the sales and support I expected right out of the gate, so my writing is shit. My writing is shit so it isn't what I am here to do. I need to find something else.*

There is a notion stating the Universe supports your every endeavor. It will always tell you when you are on the wrong path. It will, I passionately believe that.

So why aren't we always following the path of our highest good, the path we are meant to?

Because we don't fucking listen to the Universe.

This is like an accumulation of everything I have written about prior, all of them coming together, to bring this deep awareness.

When we aren't listening because we are distracted by the shiny, background noise of the world, we can veer too far down the wrong path.

The Universe, Spirit, is made of love, gives us love, and sometimes has to lovingly redirect us. We have a hard time perceiving something like physical and emotional pain as an act of higher love, but that is exactly what it is.

I was too far away from the one thing that fills me with hope, wonder, awe, and a sense of purpose: Writing. It fills me with love. Love for myself and for the world. It fills me with hope. Hope for a better life, a brighter world, and my lessons making a difference for someone else facing similar battles I faced.

If it were not for the stigmata experience, I would not have come face to face with doing an inventory of my life. I would not have found myself back in the space of wanting to burn everything to the fucking ground and flipping the ashes off as I walked away.

It was six days prior to the stigmata experience, I found myself at my office desk, my fat cat Bella on my lap, and I was in tears. I made a TikTok to share the emotions and the lesson with my followers.

What I spoke about was how all I wanted was to write. I had lost my way, and all I wanted was to touch the inspirational flow state I feel sitting here as I am now, writing.

Bringing lessons into the world, bringing truth to the confusion, bringing light into the darkness as though I am the figure on the Hermit Tarot Card, holding my lantern out for the world.

What I didn't realize is, I was one day before a New Moon in Scorpio. I mentioned Scorpio earlier, my astrology placements, and how transformative that energy truly is. I set intentions without fully realizing what I was doing.

Remember the warning about being careful what you wish for, coupled with the miracles, I made a decision to heal, without a doubt. It was like these two lessons were melding together like bubbles, and when they did, the Universe responded.

I wanted to write. I wanted to spend my time sharing my words with the world. So I needed a strong redirection because I was more than a little lost on a path I had been meandering too long, too far.

The Universe responded to the purity of my intention.

There was nothing underlaying it, nothing that had the intention or purpose of fame and fortune, it was simply a crying out of my heart.

I genuinely believed I would never realize why everything happened in November of 2021, and now, I am truly fucking grateful to sit here and tell you all, what happened is what I needed to get me here. It made everything a complete success.

-4-

Success isn't measured by what your children do. It isn't measured by whether or not you have lived up to your parents before you, and it sure as fuck has nothing at all to do with money. Success is measured by the level of joy you feel every single second of every single day.

It is measured by the laughter that rolls from you. The sighs of your tastebuds dancing with delicious food people tell you that you shouldn't eat. Success is measured in the way you allow yourself to love yourself and others. It is about living happily regardless of your house, job, or car.

Success is about living for you and showing your children how to do the same. It isn't about selfishness, but self-love. It is about living for what you know is right for you without obligation of another human being because you are too scared and/or lazy to try to make your life what you want it to be. What a tall order all of this seems for you, for me, for us all.

We are all a generation of people that never learned how to grow up. We all had to learn how to be adults in a world our parents didn't know and had no real frame of reference. Our generation and our parents' generations are so different it is like a German speaking Urdu to an American who only understands Portuguese. It's a cluster fuck of communication errors that were not conducive for the kind of emotional and spiritual support needed.

Much of my adult life has been relearning things I should have learned when I was a child. As a teenage parent who got married at nineteen, I was forced into adulthood by my own actions and mistakes. I wasn't afforded the opportunity to learn how to make a mistake without being terrified of the overwhelming consequences.

Now I have had to learn it is okay to make a mistake even if it induces a panic attack and day in bed crying incessantly because I have to perpetually transmute all the fear. I do it though, and you know what, I am still sitting here writing and talking about all the fucked-up shit in the world and in my life, and I am a success.

I have had to learn to love money when it felt as though money hated me. I have had to use the love I felt for George as he hated every fiber of my being to teach me how to love money.

It is a laughable notion really, the ways I have found to turn his abuse and actions into important spiritual lessons. Maybe that is one of my superpowers in life! Success! Again! Woohoo!

Okay, so I am feeling a little weird this morning as I write this. We all need to learn to be weird from time to time. Weird is what will assist us all in letting go of all of the notions we had about ourselves, about what we needed to do to make our parents happy, and what we see for our children so we can just fucking start thinking about what it is we want for ourselves.

I feel like I am being redundant in what I am saying once more. Repetition is the key to learning. As I was typing, I had a lot of spirits coming in to confirm it all, so as redundant as I may sound to you all, it is important for you to remember, your success is something you have to repeatedly focus on. As in focus on your happiness every single day.

See it, feel it, be it, over and over again.

As a Reiki Grand Master, the Japanese Principles of Reiki are what I return to when I am struggling, and they all start with "Just for today…" Just for today is what it means to accept we are human. It is acceptance of our emotions and actions regardless of whether they are "of the highest vibration" or not.

It is realistic.

It is all about knowing that every single day we are allowed to try again, every moment, every second. We get the choice to change, to take the steps to shift our perspectives, listen deeper, and to love more.

Every day we have the chance to feel our happiness.

Common Nonsense

We all have this notion of what "common sense" really means. Most people think of it as the division between street smarts and book smarts. Different forms of thinking and perceiving becoming different ways of being considered "smart."

I have been working on creating an oracle deck for an entire year now. One of the cards I had intended to create was called "Common Sense." It was intended to be a way of bridging the seen and unseen, the psychic gifts and the ones who don't believe in it.

And then I spilled water all over it and lost the symbol.

There are moments where the Universe will send you a big "Fuck No" sign. That one was one of mine. It was a way of saying, "Maybe you should rethink what it is that you are trying to help teach others about." This is how I came to the title of this section.

Common nonsense is akin to the idea of collective hysteria, only this one is far more laughable. Where I have come into contact with it is in interactions with other people. I have learned what enough of high energy and loud talking can do to a crowd of people.

Common fucking nonsense is the noise levels of what people are out "in the streets" saying that somehow pull in the people who are foolish enough to fall for the lies. Common nonsense is the bullshit we all tout (myself included) about Lightworkers and having a "mission."

It is literal BULLSHIT.

Grab the torches and pitchforks.

Don't worry, I won't go anywhere.

Want to listen or are we going to have a *Beauty and the Beast* showdown here?

I won't fight back; you can do your worst and I will wait.

Great! So let's talk then.

What even is a "lightworker"? By some sort of definition, you could consider a lightworker someone who works with Spirit. That would mean I am qualified as a lightworker. The issue I have is the perception certain people have once they begin this journey, and the manner in which they make it seem like lightworking is a cute little club of exclusivity. If you aren't one of the group, you aren't special enough.

Want to know the truth? EVERYONE IS A LIGHT WORKER. Yes, even murderers and horrible people who do horrible things. Harry is a lightworker. George is a lightworker. Judy is a lightworker. They are all lightworkers.

How I can say that is quite simple: without the lessons I learned from them, I would not have become the person I am today, and therefore I would not be writing this. If it has helped you in any way, then I have helped you, then they have helped you.

Fucked, isn't it? That is okay, because I feel like there is a need here to stop spirituality from doing what organized religion did.

Spirituality isn't a closed clubhouse. It is not a place in which there are only a select few people who are special, and the rest are always striving to attain that level of status. Please stop fucking viewing spiritual teachers as the unattainable, amazing gurus who are going to show you a mystical way forward. You already know the way forward; you are simply looking to someone else to give you fucking permission.

Stop doing that.

Just fucking stop.

You know what your worth is? Do you? If not, this is where you need to realize, most of the things people say, society spouts off as truth, and so on, are all common nonsense. We live in a world of literal fucking propaganda, and we only see the severity of it when someone like Vladimir Putin goes batshit insane and begins a war.

Alright, so propaganda. Fearmongering. It's kind of like Rita Skeeter's book on Albus Dumbledore – it is all about life and lies. The only difference is, this one is about the life and lies we ALL live. Did you know that there are two keys to selling anything in the world: desire and fear?

-2-

Saying that, I find myself remembering the online "event" I attended in which someone who is extraordinarily rich, sells a notion of a dream to people. It is also someone I pay monthly in order to try to change the way we sell things and teach people – I am such a fucking sucker you guys. He told thousands of people those are the only two things you need for marketing. Know what someone desires and know what they fear.

Desires are one thing; the argument makes sense. If you aren't aware of what it is that people are yearning for, you cannot sell them anything. You need to know what it is that they *want*. What do your customers dream about attaining, being, or achieving? Get into someone else's headspace, and then make what it is they want.

But selling doesn't work when it is focused on wants and desires. Nope, in the marketing world, you have to make someone fearful. You have to tell them you are offering this special cupcake just for them, for a limited time. If they don't take advantage of this sale in the time frame, they will have to pay double, triple the price.

Classic marketing, right?

Now you throw in a new level of fear.

You play off their desires and make them see what you are offering to them is the only way they will ever have it. The price you are offering is the only chance they will have. And you know you are asking for a lump sum payment of astronomical proportions for the people you are marketing to, because they don't have the money to just throw around.

Then what you do is, wait.

You market with this fear-dipped-desire notion until the very "last" day. Now you roll out a "payment plan." This payment plan in reality means you lock someone in to paying you twice what the cost would have been for the special, and they have to pay you over the course of an entire year.

There is no way to refund them, you say there is a 30-day money back guarantee, but there isn't anywhere to actually ask for your money back. Isn't it fucking clever?

So have you figured out how I got sucked in like a fucking naïve puppy? I wanted to believe I was going to work with the right people, doing something amazing, something special. I thought they were more successful, so I could and would learn their tips and tricks, and then I would be successful like they were.

We've talked about measuring success already. Now this is just nonsense. I was fully engaged in nonsense. Looking for someone to tell me something I already knew. I 'worked' with spiritual teachers, entrepreneurs, and publishing houses, alike. They all are the same. Each and every one of them. Find out a person's fears and market the fuck out of that aspect.

Are any of you familiar with Carl Jung and the collective unconscious? Yeah, that is my "jam." The collective unconscious is where I spend a lot of my time reflecting on. Learning different ways of feeling into the things people don't say. All the truths floating in the space between words come directly from the collective unconscious.

I think of it like a library inside my head (and yes, this was the notion I developed, and Judy fucking stole so she could seem super inspired and wonderful – to which I am still quite salty about because it was her yanking my own personal meditation space, and marketing it for the world, because she couldn't come up with her own ideas – I am more than salty about it, it was a psychic violation to the extreme). One in which I sit down and meet with my guides, my angels, Spirit, and I learn. This is the akashic field.

It is different for everyone, but I have a theory it became the Akashic Library because of someone like me, a writer and reader. It was someone who accessed spiritual gifts and psychic gifts through working with words. Bam! Now the Akashic Field is a library.

Have you heard of the Summerlands? It is a magical place, a liminal space. Within the Summerlands just about anything is possible, and the truth is, Summerlands is the same as the Akashic field.

Collective unconscious per Jung, and yes, I am paraphrasing it into my words, is the place in the akashic field that contains the history of the world. Not the history as we perceive it. It is not like sitting in a classroom with a textbook and learning something someone wrote about. Something they never experienced. Nope, this is where the real history of the cosmos, humanity, and the whole of everything comes from. This is the egg.

As we move into the collective unconscious and it's depths, we are able to access the fears of all things and people. When we can access these, and are smart enough about it, we can market the fuck out of it.

WHOA!

Wait!

Did I just say that we are marketing fear?

Yep.

We are collectively engaging in common nonsense every single time we are engaged in any kind of marketing or advertising campaign. This is the whole reason I cannot wrap my fucking head around marketing. It makes me sick to think about trying to use someone's insecurities and fears as a tool to take the money they don't really have to spare, in order to offer them something I cannot guarantee the results they want for them.

I used to think it was because I was lacking self-worth. What I learned is my issues with marketing has absolutely nothing to do with anything within me telling me I am not worthy of being rich AF. No, this is about me having enough moral fiber I cannot stomach the way the world markets and drives consumerism in a state of fear. Fuck it all, fuck that noise, just, NO!

This is when I make the pithy comment about "Noping the fuck out of those situations." Except I am still paying my way through having been duped by others. Was it their fault? Nope, they sold the fuck out of a fantastical notion. That is what people do. They sell dreams.

I know of a husband-and-wife duo who call themselves Katrina and Corbin Woodville (and I am actually perfectly comfortable with telling you these names without changing them, because they are fake names), whose website and claims are some of the most disturbing and disgusting I have come across in my life.

These two people are the reason, or an accurate representation of the reason why I changed my tune on my life in general. They market fear and create trauma in people. There are way too many "lightworkers" who are out in the proverbial streets, peddling fear, and amplifying the shadow aspects of other people.

These are the people who will teach you how to create co-dependent customers so you can take and take and take from someone without ever really needing to do anything. Not only is it about taking continually, but this is also about never endeavoring to lead people into their own true worth.

I have spoken about this with my friends and family many times. I do not want to mentor, coach, or do healings or readings for someone who continues to come back to me. While I am on board with repeat customers, my whole focus is on empowerment.

Helping others understand what they have within themselves. Helping them to see I am here to guide, but they are capable of hearing messages, healing themselves, and living their dreams all on their own.

The mark of a successful interaction between me and a client has always, and will always be knowing they have learned, grown, and become who they are meant to be. It effectively means they no longer feel the need to come to me for things they are capable of doing for themselves. Just as parents send their children out into the world with some advice and hope and trust they will conquer all they set out to.

Fuck all the codependent, fear-based marketing.

It doesn't just piss me off. It literally makes me shake with barely controlled rage. This is the reason there is a financial distortion out in the world. We play on each other's fears and worries, pains, and anguishes. It is fucking sick. We are all in serious need of rewiring and a call home to see the common fucking nonsense we are engaging in during these interactions.

Katrina and Corbin, they sell something called "Dream Life," and then use a claim of "30 Years' Experience" despite the fact they are in their 30s and 40s. Working on something to the experiential degree of having clocked 30 years means you would have started shortly after being fully potty trained. People buy the bullshit because they are afraid they can't do things like heal and accomplish their dreams on their own.

The program I bought into also said some shit about their fool proof formula and how you would be living your dream life with a successful business within 90 days. You have to suck the people in for long enough that the "30-day money back" is now laced in fear as well. I bought the program and it basically said, read all this shit we read, we went to this event and learned this technique, and this is how you should do it.

And in my not so humble opinion on it, one of the members is doing all the work and the other one is reaping the rewards. There is a sickening imbalance. My family and closest friends have listened to what I have read of the energies of these people, and because I am respected here for those things, they know when I have a massive chip on my shoulder from someone, they aren't a person to get involved with.

I can't seem to get on the marketing game the way these people do. They promote bullshit. They sell bullshit. And they all have a shit ton of money from fucking doing it. The imbalance in the world had the energy backward. The twisted were rewarded because they knew how to manipulate the rules.

Yeah, well, guess what? Those ways of the energy moving it is changing. Call this my official "prophecy" moment for you all. I have seen and heard this multiple times over the course of the last year. Those who are using fear to market will be seen, those who are on the higher end financially and living in a way that promotes fear, will experience the fears they created for others.

It is sad to me because I can hear these things, and feel them, and see they play out in my clairvoyance, but I am powerless to do anything about them.

When it comes to fear marketing, let it burn. Honestly, let the whole notion of selling fear burn to the ground. Have some morals people. Find your conscience and fucking use it. We all seem to need Jiminy Cricket on our shoulders far more than we have him, and it is time for that to change.

There are a great number of things in the world needing change. This way of going about fear in society, as though it is the only way to make someone want to purchase something, it is sickening. It needs to change. When we begin truly rising out of fears, it is in the transcendence that we really see the way to move forward.

Do I know what that means? Barely. I wrote it but it is channeled and therefore, I am not entirely certain what it means, but I believe it and believe we will figure it out. Within my lifetime too.

Don't give in to the people who are peddling fear. Live for you, not for the collective common nonsense. It isn't always the easiest things to overcome. We all have hopes and dreams, goals and aspirations. Those are pieces we hold within. Pieces without a price tag.

Learning to Temper

1

Sometimes we find ourselves in the throes of emotions, being buffeted about in the winds of the discord between things our mind believes and emotions of our hearts. In the spiritual community, there is a heavy emphasis on whether or not our emotions are meant to help or harm us, whether they elevate or lower our vibrations.

In my experience, some of the worst opinions floating around in the teaching community are those seeking to get people to stop feeling certain emotions. There is this belief that to feel "lower" emotions such as fear, anger, sadness, grief, depression, anxiety, etc. it makes one less than they are meant to be. It is the vibrational theory of living. Tell this shit to an empath.

It was the fall of 2021. So many things happened in 2021, it is kind of outrageous. In the fall of 2021, I learned of someone named Aaron Doughty. Aaron is a spiritual teacher. He's kind of one of the Law of Attraction/manifestation "gurus." I began taking his 21-day meditation challenge. During the course he talks a lot about a book called *Letting Go*.

I am an author. Okay, if you are reading this, it may just be one of the most obvious statements I have ever made. I am also an avid reader. I bought the book that was suggested. I read the first, maybe, 100 pages of the book. During this, I was writing my "critiques" in the margins of the pages.

I was finding myself so pissed off at some of the notions written by the author, I couldn't finish the book. To this day I haven't been able to finish it. For the first time in my life, I threw a book in the garbage. No fucking joke here.

I was rearranging and redecorating my office space and *Letting Go* was just taking up space. I was so pissed at the notions within the book, how oppositional and sickening they were to me, I could not justify putting the book back into circulation.

Nothing against the author, we all go through something that changes the way we operate. We choose how we bring those changes out into the world and into the collective. That was his way.

For me, this is my way. And the funniest part is, when this book takes off (I'm hearing the song *High Hopes* by Panic! At the Disco right now) the curiosity level of everyone may just drive the sales for *Letting Go* even higher. Nothing like posthumous riches, am I right?

I am a natural born empath. I care too much about the world and others. I care too greatly about the beauty of the human experience to nullify experiences and limit the emotional range just because some emotions are harder than others.

I have a tendency to switch into a psychological observer mode with books and authors like this. Psychological observations structure my perception, but I am not inside the skin of, nor am I in the mind of the author of *Letting Go*. This is important to keep in mind when we are making assumptions or building a perception of others and the world without being directly involved with them.

No matter how close you are to another person, it would be a mistake to deign to believing you know their inner and outer worlds. Just be careful with how you choose to form your opinions, you may just be shocked and surprised by the truth of who the people really are, myself included.

Now, admittedly, I have not read the full book. I don't know that I could really stomach it, to tell you the truth. I have this method of forming an opinion based on the emotional and physical reaction I have to something or someone. That is an opinion which is exceedingly difficult to change.

I used to believe it was a bad habit of mine. I wasn't allowing for other people to prove their energy was lying. Maybe though it isn't a bad habit, perhaps it is simple in nature. I have an emotional and physical reaction that can be attributed to my intuition pinging like a ball, all the lights going off and bells and whistles within telling me "**THIS IS NOT FOR YOU.**"

The inability to trust my own intuition for years led me to a great many lessons in life. This meant I loved too hard at times; I was hurt and betrayed easily, and when the latter occurred, I ceased trusting anymore. That ends in a bleed outward like a pebble tossed into a still lake. Ripple, ripple, ripple out from the point of impact. It is a blessing and a curse, as so many of my gifts have once seemed to be.

There is a tarot reader, Chris Reck, whose advice whenever he pulls the five of pentacles card gets stuck in my head whenever I begin talking about the things I have experienced, the pains I have endured and the manner in which other people have been able to impact me negatively.

He says it is the card that says, "Don't show your weaknesses."

Sure, I get that.

There are a lot of assholes in the world who would take your weaknesses and turn them into a profitable moment for them. Look at any pyramid scheme, or even into many of the spiritual teachers out there who set a price on what your healing is worth to them, not really thinking about what they are truly offering to anyone. Instead of seeing things you perceive to be weaknesses, how about instead seeing them as strengths. Pieces within you requiring nurturing and love. All weaknesses hold potential, the ones we struggle with the absolute most are the ones with the greatest potential to transform us inside and out.

I could definitely go on and on about all of this, for days, for pages, for years. I won't. It would get obnoxious even to me. So instead let's break down what the hell it is that I am talking about a little more.

2

I am talking about the price of "putting a premium" on happiness. I am talking about putting a price on the emotions we don't want as though there is a sniper waiting to kill those emotions.

Do any of us want to feel depressed?

No.

Do we want to be used and abused and feel like victims?

Fuck, no!

If we never wish to feel these emotions, if we don't want to experience these things, wouldn't it be better to think of them scientifically and not experience them at all?

Absolutely fucking not!

I know I am not the only person who feels this way. There is a truth I hold to, and it goes along quite well with the spiritual concept that things happen for us and not to us. Our emotions are there to teach us, to expand us, and to prove day in and out when we are struggling with living in the world as it is, we are human, and we are part of the whole.

People will say that telling a trauma victim everything happens for a reason only serves to expound upon the trauma experienced. As a trauma survivor myself, I can tell you this mentality sent me on a discovery journey which led to a healing journey and inevitably, led me here. This again is a moment to consider perception versus emotions. Our emotions are there to teach us, they can shape us, or they can control us. We make the choice.

I have recently been faced with a seemingly insurmountable challenge of overcoming my emotions or allowing them to overcome me. Not for a moment during the struggles I have endured in the last two years have I considered not allowing for my emotions to flow and flood through me. Not for a moment have I allowed myself to succumb to the lowest ones. I have found my whole being fighting against the old biofeedback loops from who I was in the past.

In the past I would see a challenge, an obstacle and my first thought was straight to, *I cannot take this, I cannot handle this. It is all too much. I need an out. I don't want to live my life this way.*

All the wisdom I contain tells me the trials are simply that, trials. They are the opportunity for me to learn and grow.

In the moment, it is not always easy to see. For many like me, who have danced the "suicide salsa," we all know how hard breaking free from that loop is. It is like an addiction. Easy way out or keep fucking going. Every single time I have the thoughts, I have the urge, and yet I find my center and calm after a while, and I keep fucking going.

Everything truly does happen for a reason. Which means each and every emotion in existence, including the ones we don't even have words to describe properly, are a part of that experience we came here to have.

When we numb ourselves to all of these emotions, we actually create more trauma, and strip ourselves of the fullness of the human experience. As a soul living a human experience, as we all are, if my soul is here, my soul desired, or contracted, to feel, and feel it all.

Sometimes the emotions get extreme. I am one in which my emotions are powerful. They are overwhelming. They are a facet of my persona that can never be removed from me, so I learned not to shut them off, but rather to allow for them to exist within me in a more tempered manner.

Tempering ones' emotions involves a level of self-control that would make a narcissist jealous. In fact, if you remove the jealousy and replace it with making a narcissist powerless to gaslight, manipulate, and abuse, then you will find the igniting spark for me teaching myself this.

Emotions demand to be felt.

They demand to be experienced.

There is a simple reason for this:

So we may learn from them, grow through the collaboration with them, and move forward in life stronger and more compassionate.

Can emotions really have desires like that?

Well, desire is an emotion, and there is a whole reflection principle we can apply here, so, in my opinion, yes. The reflection principle I am talking about is, the person we are within and what we contain, emotions and desires, are reflected in your outside world.

There is a means of recognizing emotional manifestation in the outside world, but it requires a level of self-awareness. Let me tell you something true here, something healers never talk about: self-awareness is something that is painful to attain, and it is something that can too easily lead you to feeling as though you can never ask for help.

Please, please, understand this is a mental trap, and it is something you need to shine your light through. The best way to illuminate the way through is literally to step up and say, "I need help in this area of my life, I cannot do this on my own, please help me."

Let absolutely no person at any point in time tell you your journey and your endeavors are meant to be easy, that you aren't meant to struggle or have a hard time. Why would I ever tell you this? The answer to that is simple: your journey is one that you chose, it is not one anyone else has the right to weigh in on.

I do believe at some point we all learn how to bring ease into situations and find a flow of life containing greater joy and less struggle. I believe this, and I think we all need this kind of belief. It does not ever negate nor diminish what you have experienced in your life, but it is the light to focus on in the darkness.

-3-

For me, I found the level of fuckery in my own mind when coming into the spiritual community at large and hearing all the words being spoken. The painful fact of those words being so disingenuous in nature was something I had to come to grips with.

Speaking about struggles, some lives, some souls are here to struggle. To tell others we aren't meant to live a life of suffering and struggle is to tell them their experiences are wrong. No, nothing you have endured is wrong, nothing you feel is wrong.

Struggle and suffering is a way of learning, so we are able to transcend and rise above. These experiences teach us about the other side of the coin. Truly, I cannot tell you of someone whose suffering has not brought them some profound awareness and led them to success on their journey. It may be difficult for you to see it, but if you are dedicated to transcending it all and healing, you will be one of those same success stories.

We are all in a battle of sorts. We are battling with our inner world, but we are all also battling to be heard and to matter. Everyone, from the spiritual community to center stage at the Oscars (and yes, with the recent "Hitch Slap" situation, the Oscars are simply an easy correlative situation), is fighting with everyone else to matter in this world where we have fallen to the point of not seeing or hearing others.

We are meant to feel all of what we feel. From the anger to the fear, the joy to the love. We can learn to temper our emotions, so they become passing ships, part of the journey but not the shipmasters of our destiny. How we temper them, it depends upon each one of us.

I find I will have rage outbursts at times. When my frustration level gets to be so high I can no longer continue to repress or shove down how I am feeling. It happened as recently as while I have been writing this damn book. I am pouring out all of these lessons, these insights, and these pieces of my shadow side that have been building within me.

As I am pouring them out with the intention to share them with the world as a whole, I am finding myself reflecting upon each and every moment in which I have been emotional and held myself back.

I am reflecting back on all the moments in which my kindness and giving nature have been taken for granted and taken advantage of by others. I have found myself wondering why I always come to a point in which I scream, "I am not a doormat! I matter!"

The reality of it is, I find myself feeling these things and saying these things because I allow people to take the lead in my own life. I allow myself to be a "Substitute person." Or rather, I should say, I allowed myself these thoughts and emotions.

Repressing emotions was a habit I had to break after years of being told I was "too." My emotions were too much, my reactions were too much. I was too sensitive, too dramatic, too exaggerated of a person. Whatever someone else believed because I made them uncomfortable with allowing myself to feel fully into my whole emotional body. It was something I felt shame for after hearing enough times how "too" I was. Repress, repress, repress.

Internally, my shadows began feeding on the emotions I would relegate to the inner darkness I held. Like the Shadow fae in Karen Marie Moning's *Fever Series*, my shadows continued to grow as I would feed them all the pieces of me I was too afraid, too shameful, or too insecure to allow myself to embrace. Repression is a tricky little bitch. It took me years to become aware of engaging in it. I wouldn't know until it began manifesting outwardly.

Do not fall victim to the "too" mentality of others. If they tell you, you are "too" anything, give them a saccharine smile, and very sweetly say, "Well you can fuck right off." Now hold your head high, walk away, and feel your emotions where you feel safe to do so. Anyone who cannot handle all of the beauty and brilliance of who you are, anyone who tries to stifle or silence your majestic nature, they simply aren't seeing you clearly. See yourself clearer.

Tempering ones emotions requires a lot, at least in my own personal experience. I studied psychology, philosophy, religion, sociology, people, and spirituality just to name a few. Study became my driving force. All because I couldn't allow myself to accept not knowing why for so many questions.

The act of diving into theories, books, and research, all the while questioning everything from religion to my own thoughts, well, that brought up it's very own set of lessons to work my way through.

Curiosity of the Cat

1

Curiosity killed the cat.

We have all heard this notion at some point. At least in the world I live in, we all know this cute little saying. It is cute right?

WRONG!

Telling people, especially children something like "curiosity killed the cat," is a means of telling children to stop asking questions. Stop discovering. Stop wondering about what more there is to the world and to each one of us. *WE HAVE TO STOP DOING THIS!* I cannot emphasize enough just what level of wrongness I feel in that statement.

When we stop allowing ourselves to be curious, we become complacent. Have you heard the notion of the Great

Resignation? It is about the sense of the collective giving up on trying to make positive changes. It is the pretty title that describes the saying, *it is what it is.*

Ask David about that saying in my life. Whenever I say it, he knows things have reached a point so severe, so defeating, that I become part of the Great Resignation. I spent eight years of my life married to George, feeling as though I was stuck in that life, in that persona, in that hell. It was what it was.

George would hit me; it was what it was. He would tell me how worthless I was; it was what it was. George would cheat on me; it was what it was. It became my "*I'm fine.*"

How fucking sickening it is for me to think back to the person and resignation I lived and know it wasn't right. It wasn't how I was meant to live my life, and I couldn't see my way out of it.

George was not the first one to treat me like this. He was the absolute last. George was the fourth relationship in my life that brought trauma, control, manipulation, abuse, and sexual assault. The night I texted him to tell him I knew he was with his mistress, and I wanted a divorce was the night this pattern ended. It was the night I unknowingly set the course for the rest of my life.

We never know what actions taken are the ones that will completely redefine all we have ever known of ourselves and our lives. We never know what the clinch factor for revolutionary change is going to be.

When you are in the thick of torture in your life, inundated with situations of struggle and strife, you don't see anything else. Being conditioned at a young age that curiosity killed the cat, so I shouldn't allow myself to even wonder or fathom what else life could be like, I stopped allowing myself to dream. I didn't question anything nor allow myself to explore the possibility of anything happening beyond what my life was already.

We had children. We had built a life. I was stuck, exactly where I was. I was walking, talking, living, breathing proof of being fully resigned in my circumstances.

I didn't come from a family with money.

I was a teenage mother.

There were so many mistakes I made, ways in which I didn't learn what I have endeavored to teach my children so they would live a different life from me. When you come from a life of limitations, it becomes increasingly difficult to see the possibilities within the world. Everything is something you have to fight for, everything is something you have to strive for. I do not know, to this very day what thriving feels like.

I have come to a point in my life in which I do not want to feel these things from my childhood any further. I do not wish to have my children repeating the patterns of life that have seemingly hindered my own. Yet, I cannot seem to think and feel a truth bubbling to the surface. The ways in which I have experienced certain aspects of life, they have grown me and shaped me into who it is I am today.

We need to learn to get curious again.

To not fight against the ways our hearts challenge the status quo.

It is about saying, "I don't give a fuck about what came before. I am going to change the way my life is. I am going to get curious. I am going to ask questions of myself, of the Universe, and of others. I am going to embrace the cat because it had nine lives, so if it was curious for one, then it will learn through the death and rebirth, and grow into more from the lessons."

Contextual notions are simply that. They are based upon the context we place them in. This is the same as perception. Our perception dictates our world. I have talked at length about this with my brother, Shane. He and I both agree upon the importance of perception in shaping our lives. Though we often butt heads, it is because of a communication breakdown we work through in time.

The most recent miscommunication we had surrounded a lesson I have learned. I was attempting to explain to him. It was a stark realization of exactly what I was attempting to speak about and how perceptions really do dictate our reality.

When Shane and I were talking about the manner in which how we see the world dictates how our world is shaped, I described a situation I was undergoing with George. Something challenging for me, something hurting my children, as they ended up caught in the middle of it.

First of all, never put your children in the middle of discord between you and your spouse, whether the spouse is their parent or stepparent. Secondly, if you are divorced, never allow your emotions to dictate how you speak about the other party around the children. Whether or not George would ever deign to believe it, I have always endeavored to help my children understand both parents love them, and nothing that happened between him, and I was their fault.

I do not hate George, though I have reason to, there is no sense in allowing myself to feel that emotion. It would do nothing to assist in my growth, nor would I be being true to myself. As I have stated before, we really should be working on a live and let live world.

All that being said, there was a series of toxic situations in which George, and I found ourselves in deep opposition with each other. I did not believe it was right for him to get physical with our children in order to force them to no longer be on the phone with me. He felt I had no right to speak to them while they were at his house.

The issues devolved from that point, and it came to a head when I requested he pay for half of the children's medical costs. I had paid the full amount and sent him the receipt. It was something he chose to attack me over. In the process George utilized every social media platform in order to paint me as a bully for requesting him to be responsible and make the repayment we had agreed upon during the divorce.

Every attempt at coparenting has always led to me hearing the same thing: "It is your fault my relationship with my children is how it is. This is all your fault. Leave me the fuck alone."

This level of discord between him and I weighs on the children and on me. If I share anything with him the kids come home upset about, he disagrees with the children. Unfortunately, they are the ones who bear the brunt of his anger and outrage.

He does not direct it at me because he knows I will not allow it to impact him. He takes it out on the innocent children we created together, and for the fourth time in the seven years since our divorce, I have been asked by our children to no longer try to speak with him. It hurts them, they get in trouble, they get yelled at, they get hurt.

This is the extent of narcissism at its worst. Everything is everyone else's fault. Through a series of George's own actions and statements made publicly about me, and to the children, it became clear his perception of the world painted me as the antagonist.

He was an innocent victim of my own malice. I know my life and his life overlap only in the manner of the children, and therefore, anything else in my life is not his fault nor does it have to do with him.

Perception dictates reality. I told Shane, in George's perception, I was the bane of his existence. I was at fault for every wrongness in his life. Down to him somehow blaming me for his father Barty's divorce.

Despite the fact there was an ultimatum in place from George to his family – they could maintain contact with me, and he would withhold access to a relationship with his youngest child or they could cut me out of his life – it still somehow became my fault. These sentiments and statements made, the way he continues to place blame for his shortcomings upon me highlights his perception of the world.

Do I believe in this perception?

Absolutely not. His world is completely different from mine. We really don't live in the same world at all. I know I am not completely innocent, as none of us can stake that claim. I also know I had nothing to do with the events unfolding in George's life. I didn't bully him, but when you gray rock a narcissist, yet still have to deal with them, it leaves them with little option but to paint you in the light of their own actions to make themselves the victim.

All these are psychological principles I have studied through the years. Yet when I attempted to discuss this with Shane, he felt as though I was being egotistical to assert I had that level of power over George. What I failed to explain was I did not and do not see any of George's perceptions, I observed his words and actions, but it is not my reality.

This is why we have to allow for curiosity in the world. We have to allow our children and ourselves to question things. To ask the hard questions about whether or not something is our truth or not. If not, then we must learn to find our truth.

We are all going to run into struggles in which we see life from one perspective and someone else sees it differently. You are the purveyor of your truth, no one else. I don't have any control over your life nor your truth, those are in your hands.

My truth may resonate with something in your life, in your truth, but my truth falls within my own life and frame of reference. We all have the chance to find truth within our own life.

Not only are we able to become observers of others, but we can also observe our own life. When you are in a situation in which an emotion arises, you can ask yourself what the source within exists which is eliciting the emotional reaction.

Rather than lashing out at the world, or at another person, you can choose to get curious about what is going on within your being and rise out of it in love and forgiveness. Much of the greatest inventions in the world would not exist were it not for curiosity. Nor would there be an openness spreading through the world to those like me who embrace spiritual gifts, psychic gifts, and an open forum to discuss theories and beliefs in an effort to bridge people from all walks of life together.

Curiosity is one major proponent of inner child healing. Our inner child craves being able to ask the most basic of questions of things in the world and seek the answers. It is a form of relearning personal autonomy. For some it alleviates the fears and burdens of having spent a life feeling as though they never were allowed to explore the world or their own curiosity.

Let yourself question things. Give yourself the permission to get curious and nurture that inner child of yours.

Bloody Secrets

-1-

I was a twin, a secret I learned when I was 31 years old. It isn't as juicy as a secret sibling hiding out in the world, someone my parents never told me about. In fact, it was something I had to call and tell my own mom about. Can you imagine making that phone call?

"Hey ma, you'll never guess what I found out today!"

"Oh yeah, what's that?"

"I was a twin! Did you know you were pregnant with twins when you were pregnant with me?"

"Um, nope."

Well shit! I just told my mom she miscarried a baby. Yet, that was not what I was thinking. I was in the throes of deep revelations flooding through my mind. All the medical issues I had dealt with, all the concerns and struggles with my pregnancies finally made sense, and there were memories I had never shared with anyone coming to the forefront of my mind.

It was the summer of 2018, the week prior to my wedding to David, and I found myself at Mayo Clinic in Rochester, Minnesota. Over the prior year and a half, I had undergone more medical tests and procedures, seen more specialists, and found more questions than answers than any one person should endure.

It had started years prior during a highly stressful summer of 2015, a month and a half before George and I separated. I was at the doctor for a "check-up," or so I thought. His sister, my sister, Lana, along with my son Cooper were there with me. It wasn't meant to be a stressful situation; it was meant to be a yearly exam. Except, after years of medical issues, it was protocol to do a basic blood panel. They ran a CBC and Chemistry panel on me.

After my appointment, Lana had one for herself. The extra appointment gave the lab enough time to get the results of my blood work. As we were both seeing the same doctor, after the doctor saw Lana, she came back out to the waiting room, brought me to an exam room and pulled up my blood work.

My platelet count was dangerously low. As in 19,000. The "normal" range for Platelets is 150,000-350,000/450,000.

19,000 was not just low, it was a red flag of a red flag. The doctor wanted to double check the accuracy of the test, so she reran my bloodwork.

My platelets came back at 12,000. Low and dropping. It was the first time I was sent directly to Oncology. Do not pass Go. Do not collect $200. It wasn't the first time I would experience something for this analogy, it wouldn't be the last, as you already know.

Do any of you know the saying, "Go big or go home"? It became a long running joke from that appointment for the next 5 years with me and doctors. I didn't do anything half-ass, aside from illuminate what the ACTUAL issue in my body really was. Answers, those I didn't go big on, unless you consider listing anything and everything under the sun.

Onto Oncology I went. I was told I wasn't allowed to leave the city, and the doctor was going to be certain the office called her to confirm I made it there safely. What she didn't mention was what the actual meaning of a platelet count that low really meant. With a platelet count in the 10,000 range I could have found myself bleeding out internally. It is the blood count of a person with Leukemia and/or Lymphoma.

The doctor reran my blood, then reran my blood. It didn't increase. So he asked Pathology to take a closer look. They found something called "Platelet Clumping." So he decided to rerun my blood for a fifth time that day. I felt like a pincushion by the time I was done. The last time, they used a different colored tube, something about the difference between EDTA solution and Warfarin to thin and separate the blood.

There is a rare occurrence in some people in which they have a reaction to EDTA solution causing their platelets to clump together, creating a false positive low platelet count. However, I was told it was not a normal thing for there to have been a sudden change in my blood's reactions. Something internally had changed dramatically. My blood became the biggest concern from 2015 until the fall of 2020, as though it was holding secrets, and it was time to get curious about just what secrets where hiding.

Bloody secrets, that is what we are talking about here right? I had so many secrets within my own body just waiting for me to start asking the right questions. Living in a state of confusion and fear in my marriage to George, the state of my physical health was a point of pain. I did not want to get curious about something new. It never resulted in anything beyond struggle and arguments with him, this was not something for which I was prepared.

The Oncologist called me at home after getting the latest results back from the lab. I was in bed with George, having called him when I found out they were scheduling me for a bone marrow biopsy and would call me with the date.

I have talked at length about all the red flags with George I ignored. When it came to me calling him with any kind of news having a medical aspect, it was no different.

"Hey, what do you need?"

Crying, I responded with, "There was a problem with my lab work today. Something with one of my blood counts, and I was sent to the oncologist. He said I need a bone marrow biopsy because he thinks I may have Leukemia or Lymphoma."

"When is that going to be?" he responded with no affect.

"I was told I will get a call to schedule it."

"Okay, I have to go back to work. Bye."

He hung up, and that was that. It was what it was. Despite being married, I felt utterly alone and unimportant. My mind was whirling with "what ifs" mixed with how I shouldn't even really care. Maybe this was the big finale to my life, the release from the torturous prison of living in hell with George day in and out.

After all those emotions and thoughts began, in came the guilt. Cooper was still a baby, just barely 2-years-old. Izzie was just about to start first grade, and Hayley was in fifth grade, how could I justify thinking of release from life with three tiny humans I brought into the world dependent upon me?! What kind of mother was I?!

Stressful moments in life will test us the most, but they will also teach us the most, if we remain open to the lessons. I should have listened deeper and allowed myself to be led fully on the journey Spirit was trying to illuminate for me. Simultaneously, I feel completely certain I went on the exact journey I needed to.

The call from the doctor brought both relief and fear of what was to come.

"Hello, is Monica available?"

"This is."

"Monica, I have your lab work here, and it does show your platelet count up at 117,000. It is a little lower than the low-normal end of the spectrum, but not as severe as the EDTA tests showed. There were some other concerns I have found as well. It would seem you have large platelets, and the change of your blood with the reaction to the EDTA solution is definitely not normal. I think I can say definitively there is something fishy going on we need to look into."

"Okay – so what do we do?" I responded shakily.

"I have you scheduled for a bone marrow biopsy at the end of July. You'll receive all the details in the mail for pre-op check in and procedure protocols."

"What does it mean that my platelets are large?"

"Platelets your size are an indicator of an abnormal functioning within your bone marrow. They aren't aging correctly, and therefore they are young, and the counts of them are lower within your system. It could also indicate an issue with your spleen storing the platelets. We aren't certain at this point, but the first place we would need to evaluate is your bone marrow due to the urgency of the situation."

"Oh, okay."

"Don't worry, Monica, we will take good care of you. You are in safe hands."

Sure, don't worry. Who in the world wouldn't worry in this situation? What was wrong with me? What was wrong with my blood? All the wrong thought processes swirled round and round my mind. Somehow, instead of wondering what could have changed, and focusing on the fact that I was okay, I focused on all that could have gone wrong.

George's reaction to the phone call from the doctor was the nail in the coffin of my willingness to fight, "I knew it wasn't anything." He rolled over and went to sleep. I cried myself to sleep. It was my life. More bloody secrets.

I didn't go through with the bone marrow biopsy in 2015. George was working at the North Dakota State Fair on the day it was scheduled, and he needed our one vehicle. I had to cancel. His work schedule trumped my medical appointments.

Fast forward again to 2018. I was down at Mayo clinic with my mom. They had sent me to see a Hematological Oncologist. After two bone marrow biopsies showing some unusual cellular changes, but not quite enough for a cancer diagnosis, seeing every Hematologist in the state of North Dakota in order to satisfy my insurance's allowance for coverage outside of the state, there I sat being told despite all the growing concerns, it was not cancer.

It is the strangest thing, fighting to find an answer, undergoing painful procedures, exploratory surgeries, and the mounting fears of something being missed, to feel let down by not receiving a cancer diagnosis. Even my mom felt similar to me. Neither one of us was hoping for cancer, we were praying for answers. We didn't know we would be receiving them in the following days. Answers that would lead to me learning I was a twin.

3

Common Variable Immune Deficiency. In short terms, it means your immune system is broken, defunct, and just won't work. It's like having a lazy fucking system that needs to be at the top of its game, all the time. My immune system had no game, and not only no game, but the back-up squad also didn't have game either. I had a double bonus immunodeficiency.

In December of 2015, I had one of many gynecological surgeries. This time it was a tubal ligation. I was newly divorced, had three children, and despite only being 28, I was done with having children. Right before they took me back to have surgery, they offered me the pneumonia vaccine.

It should have been something I questioned. This wasn't a normal vaccination offering for a woman in her late 20s. I didn't question it, but I did get the vaccine.

Are you guys picking up on a pattern of behavior from my past? I wasn't allowing myself to get curious. *Curiosity killed the cat*. I was not going to ask questions in the midst of life's chaos swirling all around me, all the time. Get the shot. Get the surgery. Cross small worries off my list, and don't look into anything.

The Universe continually presents us with opportunities for growth, revelation, and deep changes. These were opportunities I could not see, I could not understand, and I was not able to even engage with because I was firmly in survival mode.

Survival mode is arguably one of the biggest blockages we will face on the spiritual journey. In the state of survival, we are not able to hear anything beyond the thrumming of continual anxiety flowing through our blood.

Biologically speaking, I was living my life from 2015 through 2020 fueled by cortisol and sweet white wine. Realistically, I wouldn't suggest this way of living. It wasn't the best idea for me, and despite the fact I have said, and maintain, I am not making judgements upon anyone who is in the stage of needing to drink, it isn't something I would suggest diving into either.

I learned a lot about what the bottle did to me and for me. I learned about what my fears in life were, and what insecurities dominated my actions. I learned what my father lived through, and then I learned about my own inner strength and willpower.

The biological aspect of it all, cortisol flooding me continually was from living in a perpetual state of fight-or-flight. Survival mode fuels fight-or-flight within the body and the brain. Neither fight nor flight are a healthy way of living, however, I lacked the awareness of another way for many years.

Had I questioned, I would have perhaps been able to prevent the medical journey I embarked upon. Hindsight is 20/20. This means we are able to look back and see things far more clearly, but it doesn't mean we have done anything wrong.

It means we are able to learn so we may see the success of our growth from what has transpired in our past. What I wasn't aware of was the vaccine was offered to me due to a medical flag on my file indicating a condition known as Specific Antibody Deficiency.

Specific Antibody Deficiency was by body's Olympic team. Those pieces of my immune system chosen to fight specific bacteria and viruses. My specialists and my primary team within my immune system did not work. I had no clue, the doctors did not disclose the information, and I did not question anything.

Over the course of three years, my blood work continued to show low platelets, coupled with new symptoms, and a sudden pattern of illnesses necessitating seeing Oncology, Hematology, Gastroenterology, Cardiology, Gynecology, and Primary Care doctors on a regular basis.

Going down the medical rabbit hole was one of the most fear-inducing trips of my life. By 2018, I was at a do or die place in my mind and heart. I was either going to find answers and a diagnosis, or I was going to throw in the towel and accept I was going to die.

I was about to get married, start a new part of my life, close the chapters of my past, and I was determined to go into it with medical transparency. It was the second week of July when I was diagnosed with CVID, Specific Antibody Deficiency, and a trapped nerve in my abdomen due to the multitude of abdominal surgeries I had in my life.

The treatments for these three diagnoses involved having shots of lidocaine and steroids in my abdomen every 8 weeks as well as once a month trips to the local Cancer Care Center for Immunoglobulin infusions.

These infusions had specific guidelines of how to administer, what comes before administration, and what the risks are. The biggest risk to these infusions: Aseptic Meningitis.

I may not have been diagnosed with cancer, but I still found myself in the position of chemotherapy patients, only for me, it was a lifelong tether to this way of living.

The defeat, the sense of being trapped within a broken body, it was all so overwhelming. The pressure of being trapped was what launched me directly into questioning what was going on.

The conditions I was diagnosed with were considered hereditary. No one else in my family had these illnesses. Unfortunately, and this just happens to be another theme in my life, there was a miscommunication with the orders put in for my immunoglobulin transfusions. This miscommunication and the chain of events delayed my asking the right questions, it delayed finding any answers.

Two doctors submitted the orders. One was an Oncologist. The other was an Immunologist. If you pause for a moment to consider which specialist's orders should have been the primary orders, you'll figure out which one was ignored.

The nurses went based on the Oncology orders. Understandable, really. We were in the Cancer Care Center, and out of sheer habit, Oncological orders were what they dealt with. The first month left me drained, in pain, and dealing with a three-day headache. The second month, all hell broke loose in my body.

September of 2018, as I sat in a reclining chair, trying to read while three nurses tried to start my IV, I plastered a smile on my face and blustered the fuck through the apologies.

"I'm so sorry! I usually don't struggle this much!"

"Don't worry, I am a hard stick. I'm used to this."

The second nurse tried twice, blew a vein, and as an instant bruise started to spread up my forearm, I swear I thought she was going to start crying. I laughed it off, told her I was just fine, despite the pain coursing through my arm.

A hot pack, a few firm slaps to my hand, and the third nurse won the gold medal. The IV was finally in and saline flooded my veins, cooling the burn from the blown vein, and creating a chill through my body. It was time to start the medication.

I was the only person getting these infusions. It was something completely unfamiliar to the department, and to the pharmacy. When the pharmacy sent down the immunoglobulin medication, they sent extremely long tubing.

Now there were two options, delay the administration of the medicine, call for shorter tubing, and then get it going, or try to make it work. The nurse chose the latter. When she came to check on me, the saline was running quickly, the immunoglobulin slowly.

Again, it boiled down to the orders they were working with. The infusions were meant to take 6 to 8 hours. When the nurse came to check, the orders stated it was meant to run over

2. Now, without getting into the finer details of all of this, let's use an analogy.

Say you are standing in the middle of the street, and you know there is a bus coming. If the bus is driving the speed limit, you have time to get out of the way. If the bus is driving as though on a highway, well, you're likely to experience Regina George's fate.

I was Regina George. The nurse consulted with a second nurse, and it was decided to clamp off the saline, stopping it entirely, raise the bar holding the medicine as high as possible, and open the flow of immunoglobulin completely. I walked out an hour and a half later, went home, and knew within two hours I was fucked.

-4-

I had begun a new job working from home. Training was required at 100% attendance. I could not afford to miss time to go to the doctor. I was sitting at my computer, in training, with all the lights off, a cold compress on my head, and breaks were spent throwing up.

My neck was stiff. Stiff is an understatement. It was in excruciating pain, and my head would blow up in throbbing pain as though my blood was sludge moving through my veins, every pump of my heart forcing it to tear its way through my circulatory system. There was nothing but pain.

Thankfully, my children had their yearly well-child exams on the third day of my hell. When Dr. Binning came into the exam room, the first thing she noticed was I had the lights off, with my hands covering my eyes. The kids were snuggled up with me, knowing mom had a migraine, so they were being careful to be quiet.

I am going to stop to mention just how amazing my kids truly are. They always consider what is going on with my health, and they have learned to be considerate and to flex with me when there is an illness occurring. They lived so many years of mom being sick, but they have such beautiful, giving hearts, and are deeply compassionate. We discount children far too often in the world, but I have found through being a mother, we all can stand to learn about the decency and love of humanity from our children.

Dr. Binning gently scolded me for not coming in earlier, squeezed me onto her books, and told me what I already knew was going on. I had Aseptic Meningitis. Izzie and Cooper were terrified and crying. I was terrified and crying. Dr. Binning called David. He was to come pick us up because I was not safe to drive with my meninges in my neck as locked up as they were. It was David, or I was going to the hospital in an ambulance.

Go to the ICU. Do not stop at the Emergency Room. Do not pass Go. Do not collect $200.

I was admitted directly to the ICU, put into a clean room requiring full PPE (personal protective equipment) for anyone entering the room, and I had to be in one of the special rooms with its own airflow system. This was serious. I was not scared, I was bone-deep, soul-deep fucking terrified. I was also seriously dehydrated. My veins not just a hard stick, but damn near impossible.

Two phlebotomists on each arm were working to get no less than 25 different tubes of blood for every test imaginable. They had to call in a flight nurse and an ultrasound machine to map my veins in order to get the proper IV access. One in the crook of my right elbow, the other in my chest. I was bruised up both my arms, veins blown in both my hands, and there was blood all over the blankets from my elbow when they finally were able to get access from the rush of the blood they had cut off to get the IV in.

Then there was the issue of me having metal daith piercings in my inner ears, a homeopathic piercing I had gotten to help with migraines. They worked like a charm, but it required a pair of pliers to remove them. The doctors needed to run an MRI. We were unable to remove the earrings, so they settled for a CT scan. Down we went, and then back to the ICU. When I got settled back in bed, it was time to dose me to high heaven because the anesthesiologist was there.

Have you ever seen a spinal tap needle? I knew how long they were. Two years prior I was working as a CNA in the very hospital I was a patient in. I had seen the needles on a daily basis in the OR. I demanded they drug me as soon as I found out a spinal tap was non-negotiable. No way was an 18-inch needle going into my lower back without some sort of medicine to keep me calm.

It didn't take much convincing; they had already put the orders in for it. The anesthesiologist who was there was not the one I would have chosen. He was the one on call, and the one with the reputation of "Get the job done as quickly as possible," and while that may have been a good thing in another profession, it didn't serve for bedside manner. No one wants a quick spinal tap.

David had stepped out for five minutes, making sure the kids were okay, and my sister was not too overwhelmed as she was staying at the house with them while he was at the ICU with me.

Five minutes.

From him stepping out, to when he came back, the anesthesiologist came in, dosed me, and David came back to hear me screaming in agonizing pain.

I do not envy any person in the ICU that night. It took two attempts to get spinal fluid. I was in excruciating pain. Screaming was the only thing I could do. There were two nurses holding both my hands and holding my neck in the required position. My whole body was on fire in pain unlike any I had experienced before.

Once it was all said and done, the dressings secured on my back, and the doctor left to rush the spinal fluid to the lab, David was able to come back in. One look and I could see how hard it was for him to be kept out of the room as I endured the pain alone. I could see how much pain it caused him to see me in the pain I was in.

The drugs finally kicked in and the room began to swim. There was another flurry of activity of which I was barely aware. David stayed for a short while longer as my eyes grew heavy, closing as tears continued to fall.

It was around 2 am when I awoke screaming again.

I couldn't breathe!

I couldn't swallow!

I was choking!

My skin was on fire!

There was so much confusion swirling all through me. I had no clue where I was, and then the memories from the day before hit me. All the while I was still screaming. Nurses crashed into the room. I heard a gasp and yelling.

"Get the doctor on the phone! NOW!"

There is a protocol for meningitis patients. Regardless of whether it is bacterial, viral, or aseptic. All patients are treated with meningitis antibiotics and antivirals immediately. One of the medications given was Vancomycin. It is the cream of the crop anti-viral medicines. I had never received it before, so there was no way to know I was allergic to it.

One of the more common reactions, which can happen with too high of a titration flow rate, is called Red Man Syndrome. This is where your skin flushes bright red.

I had Red Man Syndrome.

I also had anaphylaxis.

There were hives the size of cherry tomatoes and growing all over my skin and my throat was closing. If it hadn't been the ICU, I would have gone into shock. They were quick and efficient. Reversed the Vancomycin, and then dosed me to high heaven with Benadryl. The doctor ordered morphine directly after that.

If you have ever had a spinal tap, you know, you never bolt upright. You do not change positions quickly. Your natural flow of spinal fluid has been compromised, and this equilibrium change leads to severe pain through the spine, neck and head, and it induces a migraine akin to having your head explode internally. My brain felt like it was boiling in a vat of pain. The morphine was a boon. An offering for a night from hell.

I was discharged the next morning after testing confirmed it was aseptic meningitis. Side effect of an infusion gone wrong. I was scheduled with my immunologist later that day.

Many of us go through life wanting to be special. We want to know we are unique and unlike anyone else. It is a deep desire to be seen for who we are, and to know the person we are is a mythical unicorn. I am not actually making a joke here. We all want to be that unicorn in the world, we just don't realize we already are.

I never thought the desire I had to be different and uniquely me would involve hearing time after time all about how *weird* my body and health situation was. When I met with my Immunologist after my night in the ICU, I found myself wishing something completely different.

I wanted to be "normal" like everyone else in the world. Of course I am generalizing the health of the world, but there was a sense of deep separation between me and the rest of the world.

My doctor sat in the chair next to me, befuddled, and said, "I have never seen anyone have a reaction to this medicine. There was about a 0.1% chance of you getting aseptic meningitis. You're some sort of unicorn. We're going to try a different kind of medicine. It will be subcutaneous, and you will be able to do it at home. I am going to set everything up for you, and we will check in monthly for the first six months to make sure it is going well for you."

That was NOT the kind of unicorn I wanted to be! Have I made the point of perspective clear through all of this yet? This whole clusterfuck of a medical situation was about perception.

I wanted to be special, but I needed to see myself as special despite any outer appearance. Not only outer appearance, but I also needed to stop measuring who I was and whether I mattered in the world based on what societal standards were.

After my divorce I posted on my Facebook page often about my insights and revelations. I tried to be a light for others, except the words I would post were empty. I was stating beliefs of myself and others I didn't believe, at least not about myself. I wanted to believe them, and so I used my classic method of "if – then" mentality. If I said these things and others responded positively, then it would mean they are true.

I was spiritually bypassing, attaching my worth to the reactions and words of other people, giving the background noise power over me. Right up until the fall out of another of one of the most important friendships of my adult life happened the day after my wedding.

Never try to set up two of your best friends. Here's the thing, if they are exactly right for each other, the universe will bring them together on its own. It really doesn't need any of us interfering with it, because it knows far better than we do.

David and I met on our own, only to discover my best friend, Alex, was also a friend of his. He had known her longer; I knew her better. To this day Alex and I will still ruminate on the wondrous way David and I found each other, came together, and ended up married without her ever having been the bridge between us. It was pure magic.

I, on the other hand, was meddlesome. I wanted to set Alex up with another guy best friend of mine. They shared the same name, and I loved them both, and for some reason I believed they were meant to be together. I was dead wrong, and never should have gotten involved. What happened, happened exactly as it was meant to. After things went south with my friends, there was a division between me and my guy friend.

The implication was clear, I was expected to take sides. The night of my wedding, as we all got together for drinks and a bonfire, he pulled me aside. He wanted to "dish" about Alex. He wanted me to be indignant for him, to see from his perspective, and to talk shit about her.

I refused to do so. She had been my rock through the darkest nights of my life over the prior 8 years. I trusted her and her judgement. She is one of my greatest teachers in life. Teaching me about loving myself for who I am without needing to be anyone else. She never once saw a flaw within me and is deeply loyal.

I stepped away from the conversation for five minutes, returned to my living room to see him driving away. The next morning I receive a text message from him saying, "You already have one Alex in your life, you don't need two."

He cut me out of his life completely. It destroyed me, but I didn't chase him. I didn't try to make him see reason. I spent the first six months of married life feeling as though I had gone through a massive breakup. David holding me through the tears as I overcame the habit of texting my friend to share my life.

I came to find out, he was not who he made himself out to be. He did the same thing with Alex regarding me as he did with me and her. Wanted her to talk shit about me because I was vocal about my life. Because I shared my voice and my story with the world. I let his actions shut me down. I became far more private of a person. I did not talk about what I was going through, and I stopped reaching out for support during hard times.

All the duplicitous actions others take against us because they do not want us to be who we truly are. Why they do this is because they want to be the only unicorn. I would have allowed him to have the stories I was sharing if it spared me from the emotional turmoil. I really would have. Back then at least. Now, I see all I went through as the moments which shaped me into the strong, resilient woman I am today.

These were the things that strengthened me for the biggest discovery of my life: I am a twin. Remember the guidelines for a random writing from Monica? Here is where we have gone in a wide arcing circular story so we could come back to the start.

-6-

After having aseptic meningitis, I started the subcutaneous infusions. The complications of the new medication wouldn't make themselves known for nearly six months. I was back at the Cancer Care Center monthly, only this time it was for what are called Migraine Cocktails. I would spend two hours, once a month receiving IV medications and fluids to help with the severe migraines from the damage done to my meninges.

January of 2019, in the middle of one of my work shifts, I had to take myself out of the queue for taking phone calls without being able to notify my supervisor to run to the bathroom and throw up profusely. My lower left abdomen was exploding in pain. I felt as though I was dying. It was deeply reminiscent of being 13 right before having my appendix removed, only this was on the opposite side.

I had already had a hysterectomy in 2017 due to stage one Uterine Cancer developed after high-risk HPV and Adenomyosis, the condition labeled as the "evil twin sister" of Endometriosis. Once more I called David, after sending a message to my boss, to tell him I needed to go to the emergency room.

Guilt would course through me as I apologized profusely every time I would have some sort of medical crisis. Remnants of fear and insecurity from my marriage and divorce from George.

I found out I had an ovarian cyst that ruptured on my left ovary and was referred to Gynecology. I sat in the office talking to the same doctor who had performed my hysterectomy, bawling like a baby because I felt as though I was being parted out at this point.

We had to remove the ovary. Despite the imaging not showing anything abnormal, for the fourth time in a year, I had suffered a horribly painful ovarian cyst, and this time it ruptured. The imaging was missing something, and we couldn't take any more risks.

After the surgery, the doctor came into my recovery room with pictures from my two ovaries. My right one was pristine. My left ovary was encased in scar tissue, fused to my abdominal wall and covered in cysts, inside and out. Imaging had definitely missed something major.

The week prior to my surgery in mid-February I had my second to last immunoglobulin, subcutaneous infusion. Remember that 0.1% chance of getting aseptic meningitis? There is also a very minimal risk of contracting a latent virus while getting immunoglobulin therapy. The virus I contracted was Cytomegalovirus, or CMV. It is one of the herpes viruses that can cause mononucleosis. It also can cause CMV colitis.

Two weeks after my surgery, I could barely move without excruciating pain in my lower left side. It felt like my insides were being torn apart every time I would shift from left to right, get in or out of the bath, or step wrong.

Back to the doctor, and another trip directly to the hospital for emergent imaging of my abdomen. It was my twenty seventh CT scan in three years. Which is two more than medically advised for any person in a lifetime. Every subsequent radiological imaging exponentially increases the risk of cancer development. Slowly, over time the medical field itself was running out of ways in which they were able to help me. This journey had started back in 2009, and it had been one of the longest decades of my life.

CT results were in. My colon was inflamed, and they ran blood tests. They found I had contracted CMV and the stress upon my body from the surgery caused the latent virus to become active once more. There was nothing we could do to treat it. It was a virus, it needed to run its course.

I felt as though my life was running its course.

When was this going to end?

What was going on?

Why was this happening to me?

It is at our lowest moments we find ourselves at the biggest challenge of our lives. Will we climb our way back up, fight another day, keep putting one foot in front of the other with the belief it will change, we will get better? Or will we succumb to the weight and quit?

I just kept going. Over and over again in my life, I would keep going, keep fighting, keep breathing. Never fully knowing what it was within me that fueled my fighting spirit. In this aspect, I definitely do not feel as though I am the unicorn. Each one of us is filled with a fighting spirit. We have to learn to hear it, to connect with it, and to allow it to fill our entire being when life doesn't make sense.

April of 2019, I was back under the knife. I had had a series of severe infections over the course of the beginning four months of 2019, all of which involved tonsilitis. It was time to remove my tonsils. Having tonsils removed as a kid, well it is portrayed to be a vacation of popsicles and ice cream. As an adult, it is hell. Less than a week after my surgery I was coughing up thick orange discharge.

You are not supposed to cough anything up after a tonsillectomy. The risk of tearing the stitches in the back of your throat and bleeding out is incredibly high. It is truly a dangerous surgery.

Yet, if I had not coughed it up and out, I would have suffocated. I called the doctor on Friday morning, telling them what was going on and I knew I had pneumonia. I asked to see the doctor in the hopes of avoiding going to the emergency room for the billionth time in my life.

The nurse curtly told me I needed to stop coughing. Stop coughing stuff up and stay off of WebMD. I was livid with the dismissal. I could barely talk. I wasn't supposed to talk, yet I had had pneumonia over a dozen times in the prior year. I knew what it felt like, and post-op pneumonia is nothing to mess with. I was stubborn and was going to wait until Monday to go to see Dr. Binning instead.

By Sunday, I was spiking a high fever and the coughing was getting severe. I had no other choice but to go to the ER. Sure enough, by the time I got there I had double lung, lower lobe pneumonia. They gave me IV antibiotics and attempted to give me morphine so as not to exacerbate my throat with oral pain meds.

This was when we learned I had developed a sudden allergy to morphine. My drug allergy bracelet was becoming so full the nurses needed two or would simply write "Check Chart."

Over and over again I would go through situations in which it felt as though I was being kicked while I was down. Hope being sucked away from me, little by little each time.

This kind of living, it didn't feel like living at all. It felt as though my whole life was on hold, centered around doctors, tests, surgeries, reactions, procedures, and pain. I wasn't living, I was surviving.

To the nurse's credit, she did apologize to me via phone call, and I was informed from the doctor he had removed her from his service. As much as I appreciated the apology, I was coming to the end of my patience with the medical industry.

The summer of 2019 was consumed with a flurry of changes in a short time. Our family moved into a new house, and shortly after, David's father passed away. Extreme stress on my mind and heart led to rapid weight loss and me going into sudden liver failure. It is a summer I don't enjoy looking back upon. There was nothing but pain and a growing distance between David and me. I knew from my experience the loss he suffered, but he wasn't ready to open up about it.

I was painfully narrowly focused upon my emotions back then. This is a wicked side effect of victim mentality. There is no clarity to be gained within or without. I felt as though David wasn't there for me, but I couldn't see at the time I wasn't there for him. What stress he was under having gone through such a painful loss while his wife was also seriously ill. I couldn't see things from his perspective, only from my own and conflict blossomed.

It is a testament to the love shared with two people to endure the things he and I have endured, making it to the other side as a team. Every single moment of hardship, we have fought for each other and with each other, fought for our love, and to build a better life together. This again goes back to the background noise of other people's opinions.

I could have listened to the opinions of others, the world, the spiritual beliefs of walking away from a challenging relationship. I could have, but my heart and love is stronger. Sometimes it is in reflecting, we are able to see why our fighting spirits are within us. For were it not for the strength of love, I would not be here. I would not have the family I have built, nor the joy of every small moment shared with David and my children.

I tried to do one more infusion, trying to get my body back into a state of health. It was the last infusion of my life. I am banned from immunoglobulin treatment for the remainder of my life. This time it was idiopathic hepatitis and signs of liver failure. Then my kidneys became sluggish, and no amount of testing showed anything.

I was sent five hours away to do testing for Polymyositis, an autoimmune disorder. The doctors ordered an Electromyography (EMG) to test my nerves. This involved sticking needles into my arms and legs and shocking them to find out if my nerves were firing properly. The night prior to my testing, I was in the emergency room again. This time I had a mosquito bite that caused a severe skin infection.

It was like something out of the movies. The doctor came in, deeply concerned, with a skin marker, and drew circles around the swollen red area on my leg. After ten minutes it had spread almost twice the rate out of the marked area. Normally, this would have been treated with Vancomycin. That was out so they combine three other medications and were able to reverse the spread. My lab results were flagged because of my liver panels, and they were watching bruises appearing on my legs upon even the slightest pressure.

I was told to see my Primary Care doctor as soon as I was back in Minot but was still approved to do the EMG testing the next day. Results were inconclusive, but they were deeply concerned and threw around cancer and liver failure once more. It became my choice. Drive back home and see Dr. Binning or go back to the emergency room. I was more than a little done with the ER at this point. I went back home.

Test after test, and it all resulted in idiopathic everything. It is a pretty way of saying, we have no fucking clue why this is going on, but it is happening. At this point I told David and my mom, after breaking down, feeling more alone than I ever have in my life, I was done with doctors. I was taking a break.

Dr. Binning suggested after the hepatitis incident I do a Genome study. She said whatever was going on in my body must be something genetic they were missing. Her theory was, there was some mystery genetic condition causing me to have severe reactions to the proteins from the donated plasma cells within the immunoglobulin medications.

Bang on, that woman.

She was absolutely right.

We found out much from my genome studies. What we weren't expecting to learn however was the DNA from my saliva was male DNA. Two bone marrow biopsies showed normal female karyotype DNA, my saliva showed normal male karyotype DNA. It should have been easily discounted, if not for the fact that the DNA panel showed every single medical issue I had on a genetic confirmatory level.

I fought it still. As much sense as the genetic results made, I still fought the revelation tooth and nail. I called the lab and requested a rerun of my saliva. Same results. They ran it a third time. Same results. They offered me a new test kit. I accepted, but something within me decided to stop fighting what Spirit had made crystal clear to me.

This was how I found out about my twin brother.

-7-

It is called Vanished Twin Syndrome. Sometimes the mothers are aware of it occurring. In the 1980s it wasn't commonplace knowledge. Now studies hypothesize the occurrence rates are 25-36% in twin pregnancies, and up to 40-50% of triplets and higher. My mom did not know. I did not know. We learned of it from a tube of my spit and a genetic study. What a cold way to find out something so pivotal.

In my childhood, I had always felt as though I was a twin. I had an imaginary twin brother who used to play with me, keep me company when things with my dad's drinking would elicit deep fears and sorrows within me. He was my best friend. I thought it was a normal childhood thing. Didn't everyone have an imaginary twin?

According to my mom, it most definitely wasn't a normal thing. As a medium, I can remember times in my childhood when I would see spirits. There was a little old lady who was in my childhood home. There was something dark in my attic as well. I never knew what the dark thing or spirit was in my attic, but I was terrified of going up there alone. It made my skin crawl and I felt deeply unsafe. I never told anyone about it.

I didn't want to be made fun of. It was from that fear and trauma in my childhood, I stopped seeing. I stopped seeing my twin brother as well. My logical mind telling me I had grown out of needing an imaginary friend. Now I know it was fear blocking my gifts out.

All at once my life came into sharper focus, and my heart hurt. Everything I had felt about myself and the false belief I was never meant to be born made sense to me.

Doubt is a wicked little liar living in our minds. It whispers to us, breaking down our beliefs, creating confusion, and leading to questioning our truths. Doubt is not a welcome bedfellow, but certainly one I have had to work to evict from its rental space in my head. A medium, Deborah Romano, helped evict the fuck out of the last vestiges of linger doubt about my twin brother. The first thing she said in her reading with me was the number one question in my mind. "I am picking up a brother, and I am also getting a father."

I lost my shit. I started bawling and told her about Jonah. I had read online about Vanished Twin healing. They suggested naming the twin so you could separate yourself from what you have always felt was missing from your life. It helped me in so many ways. So did Deborah. Everything she shared with me and was shown was a healing salve to my very heart and soul.

I worked over the next weeks and months to heal from a wound I carried within my body, my blood, my genetics, my heart, and my soul. A wound from the womb. Jonah was a lesson in loss, in trust, in spiritual gifts, and in letting go.

Sometimes there are things we have to heal in our lives that are inherent, inborn, genetic. The secrets hidden within our blood. The very make up of who we are hiding truths from us. There has too long been a division between science and religion. We fail to see how the two can work together to better humanity. Much of this is based on religious doctrine. The other part is monetary.

I cannot help but wonder, exasperatedly, why it is we keep ourselves in this continual state of blindness.

There are so many resources in the modern world we could utilize to deepen our connection to our inner selves and to Spirit. So many different ways to learn about ourselves and to see the patterns of where we have as a whole gone wrong, and work to change. There are lessons and opportunities for growth in quite literally everything in the physical world.

When we narrow our perspectives, allow ourselves to be stuck in the mindsets of no help to be found, and no safe place in the world, we are not serving our own souls. We are restricting and separating ourselves. We remain victims to illusions.

Even now, as I sit here writing this, I can see the visual of the emotions with my clairvoyance. As though I am a naïve child standing in front of Mount Everest, declaring my intention to climb it with nothing more than my hands and feet. This is how it feels thinking about changing the world.

So why do we do it?

Why are there people out there talking about what experiences they have had, the lessons learned, and the spiritual awareness found?

They, and I, continue to do these things because we *believe* in humanity. I believe in each and every person in the world. I believe in the ability to transcend, to heal, to forgive, to find grace and compassion. I believe in a better world and a better life, and I believe in you.

There are resources all around you.

There are resources within you.

All you have to do is make a choice to harness these resources for your growth, for your very soul.

Change the game, change your life.

Become the truest version of yourself. Make the decision that no matter the secrets, no matter the seemingly insurmountable climb, you are going to become the adventurer of your life. Take hold of responsibility for the direction your life is taking, and give everything you do, your all.

Main Character Living

In the fictional writing world there are protagonists and antagonists. Both are main characters in their own way. What does it really mean to be a main character though? I think we throw it around as a notion, but we don't stop to think about how the collective unconscious has held to what a main character really is.

Much like the tarot's Fool's journey, or Joseph Campbell's hero's journey, all main characters undergo a character arc that involves certain aspects. If we are to stand here and say, "I am the main character of my life. I am engaging in main character living," we also need to think about what it is we are saying.

Every main character in fiction and history suffers. Every main character starts out not knowing what is going to happen.

Most main characters have a troubling back story about being alone in the world, alone on their journey, and have learned to depend solely on themselves.

Those who are in a leadership position, which let's face it, they all seem to be, are tremendously unqualified, inexperienced, and find they always have to dig deeply within themselves in order to make it to the top.

When I suggest you, "play the main character," in your life this involves more than just deciding you are going to be the leading man or woman. It is about giving yourself grace and forgiveness. It is about knowing you are fallible and allowing for your mistakes to be as glorious as your triumphs.

I have been harsh with myself on this journey.

I have been hurt.

I have endured many different situations and questioned whether or not I was the main character, or if I was just supporting the people along the way.

Have you ever felt like the ship passing in the night?

That is who I once believed myself to be.

Now I know, I am the lighthouse.

I am the lighthouse, shining out for the passing ships. They have their own story lines. In some of their stories I have been the mystical stranger who has come in and changed something, disappearing as quickly. For some, I have been the antagonist. For others we have been mash-up moments as though Jon Snow somehow found his way to Harry Potter, and both main characters spent time together before going back to their respective stories.

Whatever the role I have played for other people, this has always been about the role I am playing for myself. So too is your story all about what role you are playing for yourself. Whether or not you are living the leading role in your life, comes down to your personal power.

This is where I am going to encourage you to be like Tarzan. Strip down to a loin cloth. Swing on a vine. Make some sort of animalistic sounds through the jungle we call life without a care or concern for what anyone else thinks or feels about you.

Throughout this entire book I have talked about perceptions. Perceptions and how they shape reality. How they shape our world. Perceptions on what we are doing in our life, how it is going, what place we have in the world, in our world, all of it is dependent not only on you, but also on the collective unconscious. This is a factor too many people forget about.

Because I am an avid reader and student of Carl Jung, because of being an intuitive and psychic, because of who I am and what I am here to do in the world, I never discount the collective unconscious, the akashic field, and the ways in which the mind can play tricks.

The collective unconscious is the place I spend the most time traversing. I tell you all of this because it is time for the impact to be made known when we talk about living as the main character.

Throughout all of history, from sagas to dramas, and into romance and young adult, there has been a formula and a basic tenet of being the main character: you will suffer, you will overcome.

This means that anyone and everyone who is telling you that you aren't meant to suffer doesn't know what the collective unconscious values.

Why would the collective unconscious value suffering?

This is about growth, ladies, and gentlemen. Would you want to go to an action movie in which the leading man or leading lady doesn't have any sort of challenge, it is all easy and smooth sailing? No, of course you wouldn't. We thrive on knowing there are ways to overcome. The struggle is where you discover the deepest magic.

Struggle is about perception as well. I see struggle much the way others see the Shadow or see darkness. It is a challenge. It is the vault we must get over, if only we would open our eyes and realize we are holding the pole, muscles strong, and have trained like Olympic athletes our entire lives.

Give me a main character role of fucking turmoil and chaos because I know without a doubt that is the role of a lifetime. Those are the rags to riches stories. Have any of you read the book *Spirit Hacking* by Shaman Durek? He is well off, a guru, a shaman, a healer, a made man in a world of turmoil. Was he born a silver spoon child?

Read his book. I promise you; the opening pages are enough in and of themselves to fully support this perspective. He suffered. Suffered dramatically, throughout much of his life he suffered. Can you fathom suffering at the hands of your parent?

Can you imagine dying and then defying all odds to come back, make yourself and your life a walking miracle, and an example for all others while also throwing around pithy catchphrases like "That is so pop rocks!"

No one who is a true blue, fully invested main character in their life steps into the role without having a hell of a back story.

Don't fucking diminish your own back story.

Just don't fucking do it.

Why would you?

If you suffered, own the fuck out of it. Talk about it. Show the world you underwent hell, and you came out the other side. Show the world you are Hercules or Mulan or whatever awesome character you choose who defies all odds. Better yet, show the world you are you. Show the world the real fucking you, the beautiful unique unicorn who exists despite the world's disbelief.

You have conquered the unconquerable. You have overcome the world. You have created your world. You know the darkness. You have seen the light. You walk the middle path, and now you are here to tell everyone exactly how you did it.

Just fucking do it already.

Step into your own fucking shoes and become.

In Conclusion

Have you ever wondered how an author gets from start to finish in a book? Want to know a secret?

I am an author, this is officially my third book, and I am still sitting here wondering how I got here. I want to close it up with a neat little bow for you so you will feel a sense of satisfaction with this whole process.

You went on one rollercoaster of a journey with me, learned lessons, dealt with shit, and here we are in the final pages.

Shouldn't I finish it up with something truly uplifting and beautiful?

Maybe I should and maybe I shouldn't, but when I complete this book, when I go into the publishing phases, it means there are still going to be more and more issues I have to face.

This is the way of life.

Life will not finish up in a beautiful gift of a way, but the entire journey is exactly that – *beautiful*.

In conclusion really means, in transition. Never think an ending is anything more or less than a transitional moment, a liminal stage, before you move forward into the next great adventure in life.

All endings are beginnings, and all beginnings are a new chance for a new you and a new life. This is the beauty I can gift you with right here.

Know you are loved.

Know you are worthy.

Know that no matter what you endure, you are the hero, and you will overcome.

Acknowledgements:

I cannot give thanks enough for this book coming into being to my husband and four amazing children. Whenever I sit down and make writing and pouring out my soul my focus, they are always amazing with supporting me through the process. From listening to snippets, to giving me light as I traverse my way back through the darknesses, and everything in between, it is the love of my family that sees me through this process time after time.

My love and gratitude also goes out directly to my soul sisters, best friends, and cheering squad, Amanda and Jessuy. Without you both giving me upbeat optimism as I worked my way through all of this, giving me my daily gold stars for progress, and our Zoom calls gifting me with a breakaway from living in the world of my writing, I would be far further back in this process. You two are my personal rockstars and I am honored and blessed to have you as my soul sisters in this life!

For my family, thank you for always loving and supporting me, for always laughing when I call for permission to use your names, your likenesses, and our conversations to help reach others struggling through the same darknesses I have struggled through. Not everyone is blessed to have the kind of familial healing we have gone through, and I am honored to have been a part of it.

For my moms, without the phone calls, the breakdowns, and the pick-me-ups, I would be a nervous, anxiety ridden wreck far too often. Thank you for the love you all gift to me, not because of blood or marriage, but because you genuinely have love in your heart for me.

For my YouTube subscribers, my TikTok followers, my Facebook followers, and all other social media platforms, you all are some of the most dedicated and loving community members a woman is blessed with sharing. Thank you for sticking through the silences, the moments I was on the journeys that brought all these stories together, and for the love you all always show me through our growth together. We too often discount the people who stand beside us despite being complete strangers, but your love and dedication to me and what I am doing in my life, it is never overlooked. None of you are overlooked.

For all of the people in and out of my life, you have all made an impact in one way or another, and I cannot thank you all enough. You all have a part of my journey, my heart, and my life. My soul is full and complete, and you bring me purpose and joy in interactions continually. Thank you all.

With Gratitude,

Monica

Chemistry with Kismet: Journeying into the Self to Heal the Mind

Far too easily could my story be misconstrued as one of sorrow and pain if gazing upon it no deeper than surface level. Look to the light, the hope, the love. This is a story of people, famous and mundane alike, whose words, songs, actions, and inactions have impacted my life.

This is a story of the pervasive nature of having a life's purpose, and the journey to discover it. This is a story of strength, resilience, perseverance, and the chemistry with kismet bringing me to, or bringing to me, all I required to rise up become myself, love myself, and use my once silenced voice for all those still unheard.

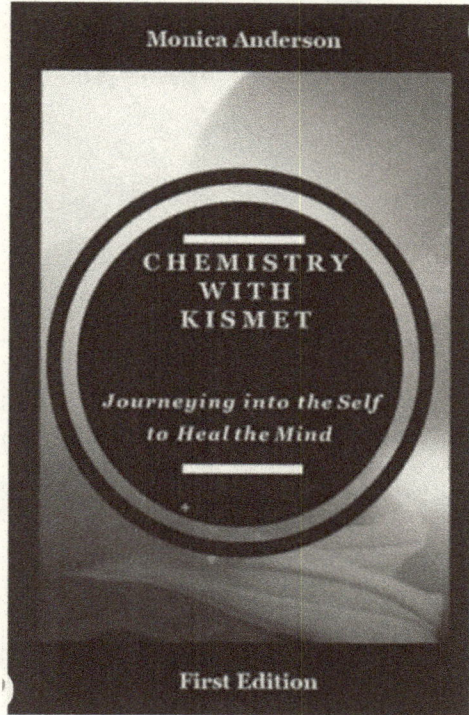

Available in paperback and eBook on Amazon.com

And What If . . . Concepts Challenging the Norm

When we as a whole look back upon the pages of our lives that have written our story, we have one of two reactions to what we find: either we are happy, or we are riddled with anxiety. Finding ourselves in a state of anxiety, a tendency to wonder, "What if?" dances through our heads as though we are unable to find the right timing and footwork to match and overcome.

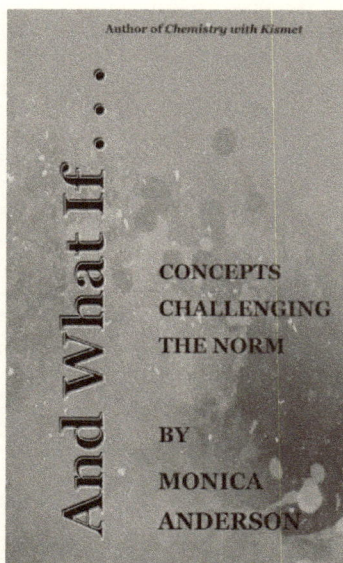

In *And What If...Concepts Challenging the Norm*, Monica Anderson breaks down common "What if," questions we ask ourselves and provides a fresh take and perspective on the way we view ourselves, our past, and our lives. Giving rise to new ways of thinking and behaving in a world fraught with anxiety, *And What If...* seeks to help each and every one of us overcome those little whatifs plaguing our minds so we may move forward living in the present moment, as our best selves.

Available in paperback and eBook on Amazon.com

www.ingramcontent.com/pod-product-compliance
Lightning Source LLC
Chambersburg PA
CBHW031938080426
42735CB00007B/182